DISCARD

Field Guides to Finding a New Career

Law and Justice

The Field Guides to Finding a New Career series

Accounting, Business, and Finance

Advertising, Sales, and Marketing

Arts and Entertainment

Education

Engineering, Mechanics, and Architecture

Film and Television

Food and Culinary Arts

Health Care

Hospitality and Personal Care

Human Services

Information Technology

Internet and Media

Law and Justice

Nonprofits and Government

Outdoor Careers

Public Safety and Law Enforcement

Real Estate

Science

Sports Industry

Travel and Transportation

Law and Justice

By Scott Gillam

Ferguson Publishing
An imprint of Infobase Publishing

Field Guides to Finding a New Career: Law and Justice

Copyright © 2010 by Print Matters, Inc.

All rights reserved. No part of this book may be reproduced or utilized in any form or by any means, electronic or mechanical, including photocopying, recording, or by any information storage or retrieval systems, without permission in writing from the publisher. For information contact:

Ferguson
An imprint of Infobase Publishing
132 West 31st Street
New York, NY 10001

Library of Congress Cataloging-in-Publication Data

Gillam, Scott.
   Law and justice / by Scott Gillam.
     p. cm. — (Field guides to finding a new career series)
   Includes bibliographical references and index.
   ISBN-13: 978-0-8160-8002-1 (hardcover : alk. paper)
   ISBN-10: 0-8160-8002-X (hardcover : alk. paper)
   1. Law—Vocational guidance--United States. 2. Courts—Officials and employees—United States. 3. Criminal justice, Administration of—Vocational guidance—United States. I. Title. II. Series.
   KF297.G55 2010
   340.023'73—dc22
                                                    2009051470

Ferguson books are available at special discounts when purchased in bulk quantities for businesses, associations, institutions, or sales promotions. Please call our Special Sales Department in New York at (212) 967-8800 or (800) 322-8755.

You can find Ferguson on the World Wide Web at http://www.fergpubco.com

Produced by Print Matters, Inc.
Text design by A Good Thing, Inc.
Illustrations by Molly Crabapple
Cover design by Takeshi Takahashi
Cover printed by Bang Printing, Brainerd, MN
Book printed and bound by Bang Printing, Brainerd, MN
Date printed: March 2010

Printed in the United States of America

10 9 8 7 6 5 4 3 2 1

This book is printed on acid-free paper.

Contents

Introduction: Finding a New Career — vii
How to Use This Book — ix
Make the Most of Your Journey — xi
Self-Assessment Quiz — xvii

Chapter 1   Lawyer — 1
Chapter 2   Administrative Law Judge — 10
Chapter 3   Legal Assistant (Paralegal) — 19
Chapter 4   Legal Secretary — 29
Chapter 5   Court Officer (Bailiff) — 38
Chapter 6   Court Clerk — 47
Chapter 7   Court Reporter — 56
Chapter 8   Legal Aid Attorney — 65
Chapter 9   Arbitrator, Mediator, or Conciliator — 75
Chapter 10   Claims Adjuster — 84

Appendix A   Going Solo: Starting Your Own Business — 93
Appendix B   Outfitting Yourself for Career Success — 107
Index — 119

Introduction: Finding a New Career

Today, changing jobs is an accepted and normal part of life. In fact, according to the Bureau of Labor Statistics, Americans born between 1957 and 1964 held an average of 9.6 jobs from the ages of 18 to 36. The reasons for this are varied: To begin with, people live longer and healthier lives than they did in the past and accordingly have more years of active work life. However, the economy of the twenty-first century is in a state of constant and rapid change, and the workforce of the past does not always meet the needs of the future. Furthermore, fewer and fewer industries provide bonuses such as pensions and retirement health plans, which provide an incentive for staying with the same firm. Other workers experience epiphanies, spiritual growth, or various sorts of personal challenges that lead them to question the paths they have chosen.

Job instability is another prominent factor in the modern workplace. In the last five years, the United States has lost 2.6 *million jobs*; in 2005 alone, 370,000 workers were affected by mass layoffs. Moreover, because of new technology, changing labor markets, ageism, and a host of other factors, many educated, experienced professionals and skilled blue-collar workers have difficulty finding jobs in their former career tracks. Finally—and not just for women—the realities of juggling work and family life, coupled with economic necessity, often force radical revisions of career plans.

No matter how normal or accepted changing careers might be, however, the time of transition can also be a time of anxiety. Faced with the necessity of changing direction in the middle of their journey through life, many find themselves lost. Many career-changers find themselves asking questions such as: Where do I want to go from here? How do I get there? How do I prepare myself for the journey? Thankfully, the Field Guides to Finding a New Career are here to show the way. Using the language and visual style of a travel guide, we show you that reorienting yourself and reapplying your skills and knowledge to a new career is not an uphill slog, but an exciting journey of exploration. No matter whether you are in your twenties or close to retirement age, you can bravely set out to explore new paths and discover new vistas.

Though this series forms an organic whole, each volume is also designed to be a comprehensive, stand-alone, all-in-one guide to getting motivated, getting back on your feet, and getting back to work. We thoroughly discuss common issues such as going back to school, managing your household finances, putting your old skills to work in new situations, and selling yourself to potential employers. Each volume focuses on a broad career field, roughly grouped by Bureau of Labor Statistics' career clusters. Each chapter will focus on a particular career, suggesting new career paths suitable for an individual with that experience and training as well as practical issues involved in seeking and applying for a position.

Many times, the first question career-changers ask is, "Is this new path right for me?" Our self-assessment quiz, coupled with the career compasses at the beginning of each chapter, will help you to match your personal attributes to set you on the right track. Do you possess a storehouse of skilled knowledge? Are you the sort of person who puts others before yourself? Are you methodical and organized? Do you communicate effectively and clearly? Are you good at math? And how do you react to stress? All of these qualities contribute to career success—but they are not equally important in all jobs.

Many career-changers find working for themselves to be more hassle-free and rewarding than working for someone else. However, going at it alone, whether as a self-employed individual or a small-business owner, provides its own special set of challenges. Appendix A, "Going Solo: Starting Your Own Business," is designed to provide answers to many common questions and solutions to everyday problems, from income taxes to accounting to providing health insurance for yourself and your family.

For those who choose to work for someone else, how do you find a job, particularly when you have been out of the labor market for a while? Appendix B, "Outfitting Yourself for Career Success," is designed to answer these questions. It provides not only advice on résumé and self-presentation, but also the latest developments in looking for jobs, such as online resources, headhunters, and placement agencies. Additionally, it recommends how to explain an absence from the workforce to a potential employer.

Changing careers can be stressful, but it can also be a time of exciting personal growth and discovery. We hope that the Field Guides to Finding a New Career not only help you get your bearings in today's employment jungle, but set you on the path to personal fulfillment, happiness, and prosperity.

How to Use This Book

Career Compasses

Each chapter begins with a series of "career compasses" to help you get your bearings and determine if this job is right for you, based on your answers to the self-assessment quiz at the beginning of the book. Does it require a mathematical mindset? Communication skills? Organizational skills? If you're not a "people person," a job requiring you to interact with the public might not be right for you. On the other hand, your organizational skills might be just what are needed in the back office.

Destination

A brief overview, giving you an introduction to the career, briefly explaining what it is, its advantages, why it is so satisfying, its growth potential, and its income potential.

You Are Here

A self-assessment asking you to locate yourself on your journey. Are you working in a related field? Are you working in a field where some skills will transfer? Or are you doing something completely different? In each case, we suggest ways to reapply your skills, gain new ones, and launch yourself on your new career path.

Navigating the Terrain

To help you on your way, we have provided a handy map showing the stages in your journey to a new career. "Navigating the Terrain" will show you the road you need to follow to get where you are going. Since the answers are not the same for everyone and every career, we are sure to show how there are multiple ways to get to the same destination.

Organizing Your Expedition

Fleshing out "Navigating the Terrain," we give explicit directions on how to enter this new career: Decide on a destination, scout the terrain, and decide on a path that is right for you. Of course, the answers are not the same for everyone.

Landmarks

People have different needs at different ages. "Landmarks" presents advice specific to the concerns of each age demographic: early career (twenties), mid-career (thirties to forties), senior employees (fifties) and second-career starters (sixties). We address not only issues such as overcoming age discrimination, but also possible concerns of spouses and families (for instance, paying college tuition with reduced income) and keeping up with new technologies.

Essential Gear

Indispensable tips for career-changers on things such as gearing your résumé to a job in a new field, finding contacts and networking, obtaining further education and training, and how to gain experience in the new field.

Notes from the Field

Sometimes it is useful to consult with those who have gone before for insights and advice. "Notes from the Field" presents interviews with career-changers, presenting motivations and methods that you can identify with.

Further Resources

Finally, we give a list of "expedition outfitters" to provide you with further resources and trade resources.

Make the Most of Your Journey

Why consider switching occupations to pursue a career in law and justice? The first part of that question is perhaps easier to answer than the second part. People change jobs for many reasons, but the reasons usually contain words like "not challenging," "laid off," "dead end," "burned out," and "didn't pay enough." But why seek a career in law and justice? The field is so vast, including everyone from court officers to administrative law judges. How do you know which of the many jobs in this field are best suited to you? In this book you will discover which skills, abilities, training, and work experiences are most helpful to those who work in each of 10 different occupations described below.

Researchers from the US Department of Labor's Bureau of Labor Statistics find one common characteristic among the interests of successful applicants for these jobs. It is an enterprising spirit, perhaps more than any other factor, that fuels success in these occupations. Nearly without exception, people who work in the field of law and justice want jobs that involve initiating and executing projects, directing people, making numerous decisions, and taking risks.

Besides an enterprising spirit, successful holders of jobs in law and justice are also attracted to the conventional approach usually taken in this field—not surprising since law emphasizes the importance of rules and precedents. Those seeking careers in law and justice must all pay special attention to the legal strictures that govern their occupations. As a group, the jobs found here require a wide variety of talents, training, and experience.

Lawyers advise clients concerning all aspects of the law that affect them, gather evidence to defend or initiate legal actions, and often represent clients in court. They refer to established law in making the case for their clients. They should be able to handle the stresses involved in dealing with difficult clients, aggressive lawyers for the opposing side, and unfriendly judges.

Legal aid lawyers perform all of the tasks of other lawyers but also usually show a much greater degree of caring about their clients, who are poor and unable to hire their own lawyers.

Administrative law judges (ALJs) weigh facts and decide disputes involving individuals and government agencies. Like lawyers, ALJs must recognize established precedents in their thinking. ALJs conduct hearings, confer with individuals to obtain information, explain how claimants can appeal rulings, and ensure that trials and hearings are conducted fairly. They must take the risk of offending parties at a hearing by ruling against them.

Paralegals, or legal assistants, follow their entrepreneurial bent in seeking information and doing research to help lawyers create court documents. Paralegals work with briefs, wills, contracts, and other legal documents that follow a prescribed form. While they do many of the tasks of a lawyer, they are generally forbidden to give legal advice or to practice law.

Legal secretaries execute much of the paperwork involved in moving a case forward. Like paralegals, they must be familiar with legal terms, procedures, and forms in order to prepare legal documents such as summonses, motions, and subpoenas. Legal secretaries must be well organized to handle the many requests of their supervisors, clients, and outside callers.

Court officers and bailiffs provide security to maintain order in courtrooms. They also assist judges in transferring documents among parties in the courtroom and maintain jury security. They must treat all individuals in the court according to established procedures, with a firm but even hand. When these established procedures are violated, court officers exercise initiative to bring about a return to order.

Court clerks perform a variety of duties, which may include preparing a docket of cases to be called, getting information for judges, preparing agendas for town or city councils, keeping fiscal records, answering correspondence, issuing permits, and collecting fees. Court clerks follow established procedures in these tasks but must also exercise initiative and direction when dealing with public queries. They must be able to manage the stress that often comes with a job where one has to multitask.

Court reporters create verbatim written transcripts of words spoken in the courtroom. They also provide closed-captioning and real-time translating services for those who are deaf or hard-of-hearing. Court reporters must follow specific formats in producing transcripts and show an entrepreneurial spirit in maintaining the concentration and perseverance needed to perform well.

Mediators, arbitrators, and conciliators differ slightly in the details of how they work, but the goal of all is to bring two opposing parties together and resolve their differences without the time and expense of a trial. Members of this job cluster use their listening skills and ability to see the common interests of the opposing parties to build trust and eventually come to an agreement through compromise.

Claims adjusters weigh evidence, make decisions, and exercise judgment when deciding the extent of an insurance company's liability. They assess damage and liability involving personal health, property, automobiles, and so on, by becoming familiar with laws, government regulations, mathematical formulas, and software appropriate to the situation. Claims adjusters write up their findings in a report that is reviewed by a claims examiner and used to settle the claim.

You can acquire needed skills and abilities that will point your "career compasses" in the right direction. The best approach is a two-pronged strategy that involves both formal education and work experience. All but two occupations in this volume—court officer and legal secretary—usually require a postsecondary degree, and even in those two occupations some advanced short-term training is often expected, either in a community college, technical institute, or certificate course. A two-year associate's degree at a community college or a similar program at a recognized technical institute or commercial business school is often sufficient to get jobs as paralegals, legal secretaries, and even some positions as court officers, court clerks, and claims adjustors.

Continuing legal education (CLE) is required for lawyers in 43 states and jurisdictions, as well as for claims adjusters and some administrative law judges. Constantly evolving technology and changes in the law may also require continuing education for paralegals, legal secretaries, and court reporters who wish to get ahead. Certificate courses are also available, both online as well as in the traditional classroom setting, in virtually all the occupations in this chapter for those who wish to advance in their field. Before you are hired, successful completion of a certificate course may show the seriousness of your intentions about a particular occupation. (Keep in mind, however, that experts generally advise against online courses in any field where face-to-face contact is required on the job, such as in mediation). After you are hired, completion of a certificate course may pave the way for your advancement to a higher rung on the career ladder.

The most reliable basic degree for any job in law and justice is a bachelor's degree. There is no one course of undergraduate study recommended for either "prelaw" students or those who do not plan to get a law degree. Any courses in which you will develop writing, speaking, reading, researching, and thinking skills are desirable. In addition to a bachelor's degree, a law degree is required for a job as a lawyer, legal aid attorney, court clerk at the federal level, for most administrative law judges, and for some paralegals and mediators.

There is generally no previous work experience required for employment as a paralegal, legal secretary, court officer, court clerk, or court reporter. Previous experience in a related field, however, is always helpful. This experience may include regular secretarial or office work for legal secretaries, or work on a newspaper for court reporters. Much training for those occupations and some others in this book is acquired on the job. Formal training programs of varying lengths are often required, either pre-employment (40 hours for mediators), or as part of the job for court clerks and court officers (one or more weeks) and claims adjustors (hours vary by company). Lawyers and administrative law judges generally have work experience built into their training, often through summer internships or, in the case of ALJs, work in their specialty, whether it is in health, the environment, or in some other area.

As you have seen, deciding whether to pursue your postsecondary education at the certificate, community or four-year college, or postgraduate level will largely determine which of the 10 occupations covered in this book you can pursue. No matter which level you aim for, however, choose courses that focus on the career compasses that best describe your strongest interests, talents, skills, and experience. The four most important skill areas, as selected by the interviewees in this book, are communication skills, organizing skills, related knowledge, and stress management. Mastery of these four areas will put you at an advantage as you transition into the field of law and justice.

Career counselors differ on whether it is better to focus entirely on your strengths as you seek a new career, or to address your weaknesses as well. Suppose you feel you are strong in all of the top career compasses for law and justice except your ability to manage stress. You might consider taking a class in this area, whether it specifically addresses stress management issues in the classroom or is something a little different, such as recreational yoga. Most of your attention, however, should probably go toward building on your strengths.

MAKE THE MOST OF YOUR JOURNEY

Once you have established yourself in the field of law and justice, it is easier to change careers within that broad field, since the skills among some of the occupations may overlap. For example, the same top five skills are needed by both lawyers and judges, as determined by the Bureau of Labor Statistics: reading comprehension; judgment and decision making (weighing the costs and benefits of a potential action); writing; critical thinking; and active listening. They are just weighted slightly differently in importance. Similarly, mediators and insurance adjusters share four of the top five skills listed above with lawyers and judges. The only difference among them is that mediators and insurance adjusters require speaking skills and time management skills, respectively, instead of writing skills. Paralegals share three of the top five skills, requiring time management and speaking skills instead of critical thinking and judgment and decision-making skills.

Once the interviewees in this book made the switch into a career in law and justice, it is also instructive to see the factors that helped them achieve success in their new field. One female lawyer cited her continuing gratitude toward those that "paved the way for women, especially of color, to be successful in leadership." This lawyer also stressed the value of reciprocal relationships, "because it is as important to give as to receive." Echoing this sentiment, another interviewee said, "I feel I am giving something back to the public." A court reporter cited her "determination" to succeed, while a court clerk and a claims adjuster, respectively, described their "voracious work ethic" and "willingness to work hard at being the best." A legal aid attorney stated, "I try my best to make sure people are treated fairly by the courts and the prosecutor."

To summarize your journey to a career in law and justice, first decide whether you have both the enterprising and conventional spirits that are typical of those who succeed in this broad field. Next, consider each of the 10 careers briefly described above and see in which ones you can comfortably picture yourself. Analyze how well you think you exemplify or can master the four career compasses and four skill areas most often associated with successful holders of the 10 occupations covered in this book. Perhaps most important, decide what investment in postsecondary education, if any, you are prepared to make in order to pursue one of these careers. Your ability to be realistic in your career goals is perhaps your greatest asset in your job search. If after this work you believe you have or can develop the talents, training, and temperament you need to succeed in finding a new career in law and justice, you are well on your way to meeting your goal.

Self-Assessment Quiz

I: Relevant Knowledge

1. How many years of specialized training have you had?
   (a) None, it is not required
   (b) Several weeks to several months of training
   (c) A year-long course or other preparation
   (d) Years of preparation in graduate or professional school, or equivalent job experience

2. Would you consider training to obtain certification or other required credentials?
   (a) No
   (b) Yes, but only if it is legally mandated
   (c) Yes, but only if it is the industry standard
   (d) Yes, if it is helpful (even if not mandatory)

3. In terms of achieving success, how would you rate the following qualities in order from least to most important?
   (a) ability, effort, preparation
   (b) ability, preparation, effort
   (c) preparation, ability, effort
   (d) preparation, effort, ability

4. How would you feel about keeping track of current developments in your field?
   (a) I prefer a field where very little changes
   (b) If there were a trade publication, I would like to keep current with that
   (c) I would be willing to regularly recertify my credentials or learn new systems
   (d) I would be willing to aggressively keep myself up-to-date in a field that changes constantly

5. For whatever reason, you have to train a bright young successor to do your job. How quickly will he or she pick it up?
   (a) Very quickly
   (b) He or she can pick up the necessary skills on the job
   (c) With the necessary training he or she should succeed with hard work and concentration
   (d) There is going to be a long breaking-in period—there is no substitute for experience

II: Caring

1. How would you react to the following statement: "Other people are the most important thing in the world?"
   (a) No! Me first!
   (b) I do not really like other people, but I do make time for them
   (c) Yes, but you have to look out for yourself first
   (d) Yes, to such a degree that I often neglect my own well-being

2. Who of the following is the best role model?
   (a) Ayn Rand
   (b) Napoléon Bonaparte
   (c) Bill Gates
   (d) Florence Nightingale

3. How do you feel about pets?
   (a) I do not like animals at all
   (b) Dogs and cats and such are OK, but not for me
   (c) I have a pet, or I wish I did
   (d) I have several pets, and caring for them occupies significant amounts of my time

4. Which of the following sets of professions seems most appealing to you?
   (a) business leader, lawyer, entrepreneur
   (b) politician, police officer, athletic coach
   (c) teacher, religious leader, counselor
   (d) nurse, firefighter, paramedic

5. How well would you have to know someone to give them $100 in a harsh but not life-threatening circumstance? It would have to be...
   (a) ...a close family member or friend (brother or sister, best friend)
   (b) ...a more distant friend or relation (second cousin, coworkers)
   (c) ...an acquaintance (a coworker, someone from a community organization or church)
   (d) ...a complete stranger

III: Organizational Skills

1. Do you create sub-folders to further categorize the items in your "Pictures" and "Documents" folders on your computer?
   (a) No
   (b) Yes, but I do not use them consistently
   (c) Yes, and I use them consistently
   (d) Yes, and I also do so with my e-mail and music library

2. How do you keep track of your personal finances?
   (a) I do not, and I am never quite sure how much money is in my checking account
   (b) I do not really, but I always check my online banking to make sure I have money
   (c) I am generally very good about budgeting and keeping track of my expenses, but sometimes I make mistakes
   (d) I do things such as meticulously balance my checkbook, fill out Excel spreadsheets of my monthly expenses, and file my receipts

3. Do you systematically order commonly used items in your kitchen?
   (a) My kitchen is a mess
   (b) I can generally find things when I need them
   (c) A place for everything, and everything in its place
   (d) Yes, I rigorously order my kitchen and do things like alphabetize spices and herbal teas

4. How do you do your laundry?
   (a) I cram it in any old way
   (b) I separate whites and colors

(c) I separate whites and colors, plus whether it gets dried
(d) Not only do I separate whites and colors and drying or non-drying, I organize things by type of clothes or some other system

5. Can you work in clutter?
    (a) Yes, in fact I feel energized by the mess
    (b) A little clutter never hurt anyone
    (c) No, it drives me insane
    (d) Not only does my workspace need to be neat, so does that of everyone around me

IV: Communication Skills

1. Do people ask you to speak up, not mumble, or repeat yourself?
    (a) All the time
    (b) Often
    (c) Sometimes
    (d) Never

2. How do you feel about speaking in public?
    (a) It terrifies me
    (b) I can give a speech or presentation if I have to, but it is awkward
    (c) No problem!
    (d) I frequently give lectures and addresses, and I am very good at it

3. What's the difference between *their*, *they're*, and *there*?
    (a) I do not know
    (b) I know there is a difference, but I make mistakes in usage
    (c) I know the difference, but I cannot articulate it
    (d) *Their* is the third-person possessive, *they're* is a contraction for *they are*, and *there* is a deictic adverb meaning "in that place"

4. Do you avoid writing long letters or e-mails because you are ashamed of your spelling, punctuation, and grammatical mistakes?
    (a) Yes
    (b) Yes, but I am either trying to improve or just do not care what people think

(c) The few mistakes I make are easily overlooked
(d) Save for the occasional typo, I do not ever make mistakes in usage

5. Which choice best characterizes the most challenging book you are willing to read in your spare time?
   (a) I do not read
   (b) Light fiction reading such as the Harry Potter series, *The Da Vinci Code*, or mass-market paperbacks
   (c) Literary fiction or mass-market nonfiction such as history or biography
   (d) Long treatises on technical, academic, or scientific subjects

V: Mathematical Skills

1. Do spreadsheets make you nervous?
   (a) Yes, and I do not use them at all
   (b) I can perform some simple tasks, but I feel that I should leave them to people who are better-qualified than myself
   (c) I feel that I am a better-than-average spreadsheet user
   (d) My job requires that I be very proficient with them

2. What is the highest level math class you have ever taken?
   (a) I flunked high-school algebra
   (b) Trigonometry or pre-calculus
   (c) College calculus or statistics
   (d) Advanced college mathematics

3. Would you rather make a presentation in words or using numbers and figures?
   (a) Definitely in words
   (b) In words, but I could throw in some simple figures and statistics if I had to
   (c) I could strike a balance between the two
   (d) Using numbers as much as possible; they are much more precise

4. Cover the answers below with a sheet of paper, and then solve the following word problem: Mary has been legally able to vote for exactly half her life. Her husband John is three years older than she. Next year,

their son Harvey will be exactly one-quarter of John's age. How old was Mary when Harvey was born?
(a) I couldn't work out the answer
(b) 25
(c) 26
(d) 27

5. Cover the answers below with a sheet of paper, and then solve the following word problem: There are seven children on a school bus. Each child has seven book bags. Each bag has seven big cats in it. Each cat has seven kittens. How many legs are there on the bus?
(a) I couldn't work out the answer
(b) 2,415
(c) 16,821
(d) 10,990

VI: Ability to Manage Stress

1. It is the end of the working day, you have 20 minutes to finish an hour-long job, and you are scheduled to pick up your children. Your supervisor asks you why you are not finished. You:
   (a) Have a panic attack
   (b) Frantically redouble your efforts
   (c) Calmly tell her you need more time, make arrangements to have someone else pick up the kids, and work on the project past closing time
   (d) Calmly tell her that you need more time to do it right and that you have to leave, or ask if you can release this flawed version tonight

2. When you are stressed, do you tend to:
   (a) Feel helpless, develop tightness in your chest, break out in cold sweats, or have other extreme, debilitating physiological symptoms?
   (b) Get irritable and develop a hair-trigger temper, drink too much, obsess over the problem, or exhibit other "normal" signs of stress?
   (c) Try to relax, keep your cool, and act as if there is no problem
   (d) Take deep, cleansing breaths and actively try to overcome the feelings of stress

SELF-ASSESSMENT QUIZ

3. The last time I was so angry or frazzled that I lost my composure was:
    (a) Last week or more recently
    (b) Last month
    (c) Over a year ago
    (d) So long ago I cannot remember

4. Which of the following describes you?
    (a) Stress is a major disruption in my life, people have spoken to me about my anger management issues, or I am on medication for my anxiety and stress
    (b) I get anxious and stressed out easily
    (c) Sometimes life can be a challenge, but you have to climb that mountain!
    (d) I am generally easygoing

5. What is your ideal vacation?
    (a) I do not take vacations; I feel my work life is too demanding
    (b) I would just like to be alone, with no one bothering me
    (c) I would like to do something not too demanding, like a cruise, with friends and family
    (d) I am an adventurer; I want to do exciting (or even dangerous) things and visit foreign lands

Scoring:

For each category...

For every answer of *a*, add zero points to your score.
For every answer of *b*, add ten points to your score.
For every answer of *c*, add fifteen points to your score.
For every answer of *d*, add twenty points to your score.

The result is your percentage in that category.

Lawyer

 # Lawyer

Career Compasses

Weigh the skills you need to be a successful lawyer.

Communication Skills to clarify your client's needs and explain how you can meet them (30%)

Relevant Knowledge of the law and how it applies to your client's case (30%)

Ability to Manage Stress in order to maintain your composure under pressure (20%)

Organizational Skills to marshal the arguments that can persuade a judge or jury (20%)

Destination: Lawyer

Lawyers are among the most sought after and yet most castigated professions in the United States and many other nations. How can one explain this paradox? Perhaps it is our very emphasis on the need for law that causes us to criticize lawyers when they fail to meet our high expectations. Partly because attorneys are generally well paid, the United States has more lawyers per capita than any other country in the world (1 for every 500 Americans). In 2004, lawyers were the nineteenth highest-paid occupation in the United States, according to the Bureau of Labor Statistics. Those ranking higher included 11 different categories of medical and dental professionals, CEOs, and 3 categories of airline and space specialists. The recession that began in 2007 has begun to change that pecking order, yet lawyers on average can still do quite well, especially if they fill an underserved need or niche in society by virtue of their specialty.

Practicing lawyers use their skills and abilities either to (1) advise clients who plan to undertake business transactions; or (2) advocate for clients in civil or criminal trials by presenting evidence and making arguments in courts of law.

What does it take to become a successful lawyer? One of their key skills is in analyzing great amounts of information. Other skills and abilities measured on the Law School Admission Test, or LSAT, include: reading comprehension and critical thinking skills to understand and evaluate information; organizational skills to be able to access and use information efficiently; ability to evaluate the relative cost and benefit of potential actions; and ability to communicate clearly and persuasively to support a court case.

> *Essential Gear*
> **The American Bar Association Web site.** The official site of the ABA has a wealth of information for prospective law students and beginning lawyers. On the home page, click on Legal Education and choose "getting a Law Degree" or "Careers in the Legal Profession." Follow the topics that interest you. http://www.abanet.org

Some law professors have criticized the LSAT for placing too much emphasis on analytic skills. Their research shows that other characteristics—such as being able to write, listen, manage stress, and solve hypothetical problems—are equally important, if not more so, in predicting how effective a lawyer will be.

To the list of characteristics of the successful lawyer, the American Bar Association (ABA) would add the goal of "serving others, honestly, competently, and responsibly . . . and . . . improving fairness and the quality of justice in the legal system." To achieve that goal, the ABA recommends that all those considering the law "seek some significant experience, before coming to law school, in which you devote substantial effort toward assisting others." The ABA also recommends that those practicing law do a certain amount of legal work pro bono, or without pay, for those who cannot afford a lawyer.

To hone these skills, abilities, and values, all lawyers generally complete four years of college, three years of law school, and pass a state bar examination, but requirements vary from state to state.

The ABA recommends no specific courses in college to prepare one for a career in the law. It does suggest, however, "some basic areas of knowledge that are helpful to a legal education." These areas include broad or fundamental knowledge of history, mathematics, economics, human behavior and social interaction, and world cultures and the relationships among them that have made nations increasingly interdependent.

Lawyers are needed in some capacity just about everywhere. You will find them in all branches of government at the federal, state, and local levels, and in most industries in the private sector. They may work directly for government agencies or corporate industries, or they may own their own private practices. Some lawyers work for providers of legal services to those who cannot afford lawyers. In addition, due to intense competition for most legal positions, lawyers are increasingly finding work in fields where legal training is useful but not required, such as managerial and administrative positions in banks, real estate firms, and insurance companies.

Essential Gear

Confront the law school myths. Steven R. Sedberry's *The Law School Labyrinth: A Guide to Making the Most of Your Law School Education* (Kaplan Publishing, 2009) provides a road map to this intense three-year experience, dispelling misinformation and offering advice on how to get admitted, pass exams, and begin a career.

What are the prospects for lawyers during a recession? Despite the image we have of lawyers as uniformly well paid, they are not immune to layoffs and loss of business during recessions. This is especially true of lawyers who work in or advise corporations that are subject to the business cycle. Recessions can mean a much tighter labor market for lawyers in general, except for those who handle bankruptcies, foreclosures, and some divorces. During tough economic times, some lawyers turn to temporary staffing firms where they can find short-term jobs.

Probably the happiest lawyers are those who seek to serve some higher purpose than merely fulfilling their own material needs and desires. Lawyers may serve the common good through public service to the government or some nonprofit organization, or by taking on some clients without regard for their ability to pay. In these ways lawyers help to uphold the key principle of equal justice under law that is basic to American values.

You Are Here

Your journey to becoming a lawyer begins by focusing on questions that may help you determine a career path.

What are your passionate academic interests? While many attorneys handle all kinds of cases, especially in small firms, many of those considering the law have a special love for economics, business, science, psychology, or some other area. Those with excellent economics and business sense may find the law courses in bankruptcy, antitrust, insurance, and taxation, for example, to be especially stimulating. Others may enjoy using their psychological skills to focus on classes in family law,

Navigating the Terrain

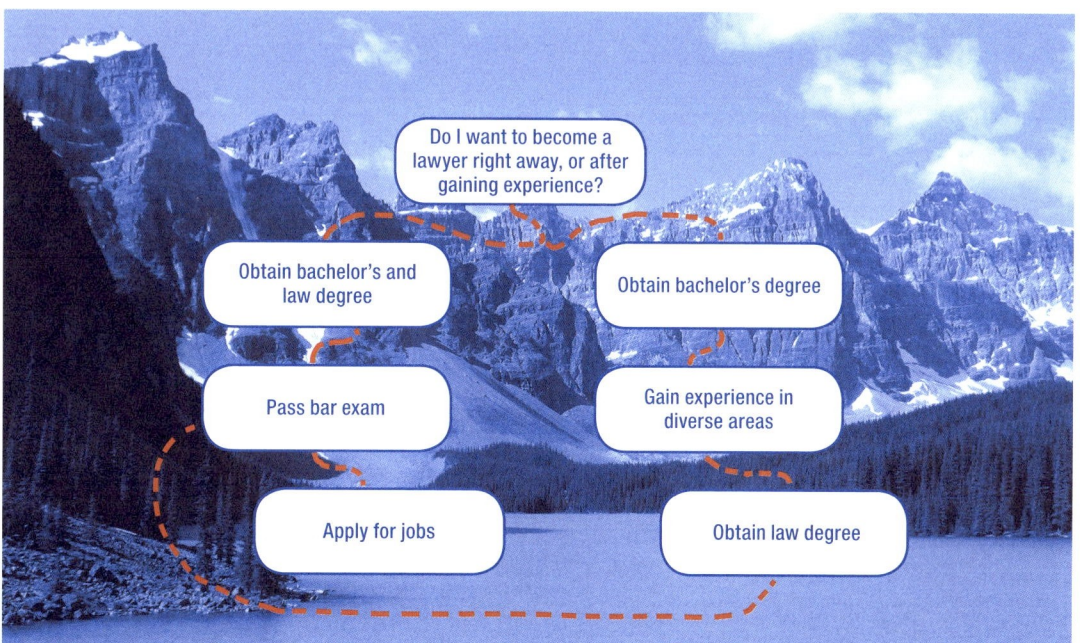

personal injury, trusts and estates, and so on. You will have a chance to investigate all these areas in law school, but the kinds of cases that really excite you as an undergraduate may be clues to your eventual career path.

Do you have work or life experience skills that you could transfer to a career in law? Those with a science background may find a natural segue into intellectual property law as a copyright or patent attorney. Experience in the financial world could transfer into a career in banking law, commercial bankruptcy, or business law. Experience in social services can give you a head start in family law, among other areas.

How important to you are your hobbies and extracurricular interests? For some of us, these are at least as important in life as our work. For example, your devotion to the arts could lead to a career in entertainment law. Your passionate interest in the natural world could take you down a path to environmental law.

Organizing Your Expedition

Before you start out, check out some landmarks.

Decide on a destination. Perhaps no other profession opens up so many potential career paths, both within and outside the field of law. Try not to foreclose on the possibilities available before giving close attention to those areas that interest you the most. If you need a break from the academic world before entering law school, you might apply for a paralegal position at a law firm. Here you can ask supervisors about the kinds of cases they handle. They can provide valuable mentoring in finding the kind of law practice that appeals to you. If you choose to go straight to law school, ask your professors for advice on the kinds of students who do best in specific types of law.

Scout the terrain. If you elect to go to law school directly out of college, the law school you attend will define your path, at least for the moment. Use your summers, however, to explore this vast field, whether as a summer associate or in some other capacity at a law firm, or in a company with a law department or one that uses legal services. Here again you can ask lawyers about the kind of work they do. This would also be a good time to use the ABA's career services to contact lawyers in specific fields (see full listing under Further Resources).

Find the path that's right for you. Through your law-related jobs and life experience, an area of law for which you are well suited may gradually come into focus. Remember that whatever area you choose, you have not ruled out other areas for future exploration. Many lawyers have more than one specialty, and it is not uncommon for an interest in one area, say patent law, to lead to another, such as antitrust law.

Go back to school. If you have had a good job experience in a law-related field after college, you should be better prepared to take on law school, for you will now have a better idea of what lies ahead after you receive your Juris Doctor (a professional doctorate in law).

Landmarks

If you are in your twenties . . . Since law school is an additional major financial burden for students who have just finished college, you may find it wise at this point in your life to get a job in a government agency, for example, where you can not only make money but also gain valuable life experience that bears directly on your interest in the law.

If you are in your thirties or forties . . . Do you find yourself at this point in your career in a job where lawyers seem to call most of the shots? If so, that realization can be a powerful incentive to go after a law degree and get closer to the levers of power, either in your old job or in a new one that takes full advantage of your law degree.

If you are in your fifties . . . If you find yourself in a job that is too routine and that offers no new challenges, then law school, either full time or part time, can serve to recharge your batteries and offer new vistas to explore.

If you are over sixty . . . For those who are in a position to retire from their current positions with an adequate nest egg, this may be the best time fulfill your dream of a second career that requires a law degree.

LAW AND JUSTICE

Notes from the Field
Ruthe Catolico Ashley
Lawyer
Sacramento, California

What were you doing before you decided to change careers?

I was an assistant professor of nursing at CSU/Los Angeles. I had been in nursing for 15 years after graduation from college with a B.S. in nursing and later an M.S.

Why did you change your career?

I was in a midlife crisis, wondering what to do with the rest of my life. On a "girls' weekend" away from our husbands and kids, [my friends and I] happened to watch *The Cosby Show*. It turned out to be the half hour that changed my life. Claire Huxtable was beautiful, lived in picture-perfect house, never cooked, and was a lawyer. There was a five-minute segment where she talked to her husband about a court case. When the show was over, I announced to my friends that I was going to law school. Within a week, I had applied. I was accepted contingent on passing the LSAT. I had no idea what the LSAT was. I didn't know a plaintiff from a defendant, and I thought a tort was a pastry. I had made an emotional decision, but in hindsight, it was the best decision I ever made for my career.

Your accumulated life wisdom can only be an advantage as you set out on your new path.

Further Resources

Under the heading Continuing Legal Education (CLE), the **American Bar Association** Web site contains career profiles of 250 different practitioners in law specialties ranging from Administrative Law to Worker's Compensation. Profiles give a basic résumé for the practitioners, with sections on how they arrived where they are, what they do, and why they do it. http://www.abanet.org/careercounsel/profile/profession.html

The **Association for Legal Career Professionals** has an online Directory of Legal Employers that features information on more than 1,700

LAWYER

How did you make the transition?

It was quite difficult the first year, but I was determined to succeed. My mother had always said, "Ruthe, you must get an education. No one can take that away from you." Fortunately, after graduation from law school I was able to use my nursing background to develop a practice in health care, medical malpractice, and professional liability law at several law firms before changing my focus to career and professional development. I also volunteered and was active in several professional groups, which are another valuable source of experience and contacts. Today I am president and CEO of a nonprofit organization where I can express my passion for building educational pipelines that will produce a diverse workforce and provide future leaders.

What are the keys to success in your career?

I have always looked for open doors and believe in walking through whenever opportunity presents itself. I believe that I stand on the shoulders of others who have gone before me, and I am always grateful for those that paved the way for women, especially of color, to be successful in leadership and in other areas not traditionally open them. I believe in building and maintaining reciprocal relationships with others, because it is important to give as well as receive. The best skill of all is the ability to listen well. The law has provided me with a network of friends around the world and opportunities I could not have dreamed of when I started.

job sources. This continuously updated directory allows for searches by practice, geographic area, and criteria for hiring law students. The NALP Web site also has discussion groups, links to other sources for career development, and special sections on public service and diversity initiatives.   http://www.nalp.org

Administrative Law Judge

Administrative Law Judge

Career Compasses

Weigh the most important skills necessary to be a successful administrative law judge.

Communication Skills in making decisions that both parties in a dispute will perceive as fair (60%)

Relevant Knowledge of the facts in each case (20%)

Caring about the individuals and agencies that come before you in court (10%)

Organizational Skills in efficiently moving forward the cases on your docket (10%)

Destination: Administrative Law Judge

Administrative law judges (ALJs) make judgments without the direct guidance of a jury. You will not often find their decisions announced in the daily press. Few people know they even exist. Yet one of their decisions may ultimately affect thousands of people. They are sometimes called hearing officers or adjudicators, and their responsibilities and status vary widely from state to state. ALJs decide how government regulations (in contrast to civil or criminal laws) apply to specific people.

Suppose an injured worker believes he or she has been unjustly denied workers' compensation benefits. An ALJ will rule on the case. These judges also hear cases involving eligibility for Social Security benefits, alleged violations of environmental laws, or infractions of health and safety regulations, just to take a few examples from the 29 different federal agencies that hire ALJs.

ALJs are only 15,000 in number, or 29 percent of the 51,000 judges, magistrates, and other judicial workers in the federal, state, and local judicial system. Of these 15,000, 59 percent work in state governments, 22 percent in the federal government, and 19 percent in local governments. Since they serve executive agencies, such as the federal Environmental Protection Agency (EPA) or a particular state EPA, ALJs are part of the executive branch, even though they perform a judicial function. States have designed different ways to keep the judgments of ALJs, hearing officers, and adjudicators separate and independent from the rule-making and prosecutorial function of the particular agency. In all states, ALJs, by whatever name, have been essential to government ever since the United States was formed. At that time, President George Washington created commissions to calculate the benefits of veterans of the American Revolution and to create a tariff system for American ports.

> ## Essential Gear
> **Approach the bench.** The National Center for State Courts Web site has links to 38 state Web sites that describe in details how each of those states handles administrative hearings. http://www.ncsconline.org/WC/CourTopics/StateLinks.asp?id=1158topic=Adm.Law

How do you become an administrative law judge? At the federal level, which accounts for 22 percent of the approximately 9,000 in this category, ALJs are appointed by different federal agencies based on a comprehensive test that includes both written and oral sections. All federal ALJs have law degrees and over five years of experience in a specialized area such as banking. Some federal ALJs have lifetime tenure in their jobs. At the state and city levels, requirements may be less stiff and job tenure less secure. Though candidates with law degrees have a better chance of appointment, it is possible to be an hearing officer or adjudicator at the state or local level, depending on the agency, with as little as a bachelor's degree. ALJs, hearing officers, and adjudicators at

ADMINISTRATIVE LAW JUDGE

the state and local levels may be appointed or elected. Their duties and status vary widely from state to state. Potential ALJs usually need experience in settling disputes either from pretrial negotiations or through alternative dispute mediation. Some candidates may also need to pass an exam and have a license to practice. It is best to check your state government's Web site for your state or city's specific requirements.

All ALJs should have a reputation for ethical behavior and responsibility in serving the public. They must be able to research information in a particular area and assess its relevance to a particular case. They should feel comfortable in working with other people, often in a teaching, helping, or serving role. They should have an enterprising bent and be able to take risks and make decisions. They should be accustomed to following set procedures and routines. Most must regularly take part in continuing education to improve their skills.

> ## Essential Gear
> **Virginia is for lawyers . . . and judges.** Virginia is a good example of a state that not only advertises jobs as ALJs but also includes a "Career Guide for Administrative Law Judge and Hearing Officer" on the state's Web site, which explains what skills, knowledge, abilities, and tasks are required. http://jobs.virginia.gov/careerguides/ALJ.htm

There is probably no typical day in the life of ALJs because of the variety of tasks they do. These may include the following:

- authorizing payment of valid claims
- conducting hearings to review and decide claims and determine liability
- meeting with those involved in cases to obtain relevant information
- explaining to claimants how they can appeal rulings
- issuing subpoenas, administering oaths, monitoring and conducting hearings
- preparing opinions and decisions
- researching and analyzing laws and other written regulations and policies

The higher the position in this field, the more competition you can expect, with appointed positions generally having more prestige than elected posts. Serving as an ALJ is not for those who feel their own personal or political views have equal or more weight than the facts of the case. Although the job often depends on one's ability to work without supervision, one must also be willing to cooperate with others and use analysis of information and logic to solve problems rather than the force of rhetoric and personality. For those who have superior skills and a strong desire to make government work, a job as an ALJ, hearing officer, or adjudicator can be very rewarding work.

You Are Here

As you investigate this career, consider these questions.

Can you be fair and impartial in interpreting government regulations in order to resolve disputes? ALJs, hearing officers, and adjudicators interpret the law, yet they are part of the executive branch, whose purpose is to carry out and enforce the law, whether at the state or federal level. ALJs must keep these dual functions separate. For example, ALJs in the Department of Environmental Protection cannot let their interpretations of disputes unduly favor particular industries covered by their decisions.

Would you rather work in an appointed or an elected position? Federal ALJs are all appointed on merit, so your experience and oral and written exam scores will be key. Merit is also an important factor in winning elected positions at any level, but you must also obtain the endorsement of a political party, so political skills play a role in your success. Many political parties endorse ALJs, so your ability to persuade is important.

Do you have a special interest in one area of administrative law? Most ALJs specialize in one area of the administrative law, depending on the government department in which they work. An ALJ in the Social Security Administration, for example, specializes in cases involving Social Security, while an ALJ in the Department of Labor focuses on areas such as employment discrimination. Other specialized areas covered by federal agencies with ALJs include: Coast Guard, commodity futures trading, agriculture, health and human services, housing and urban development, government-owned land, justice, labor and labor relations,

Navigating the Terrain

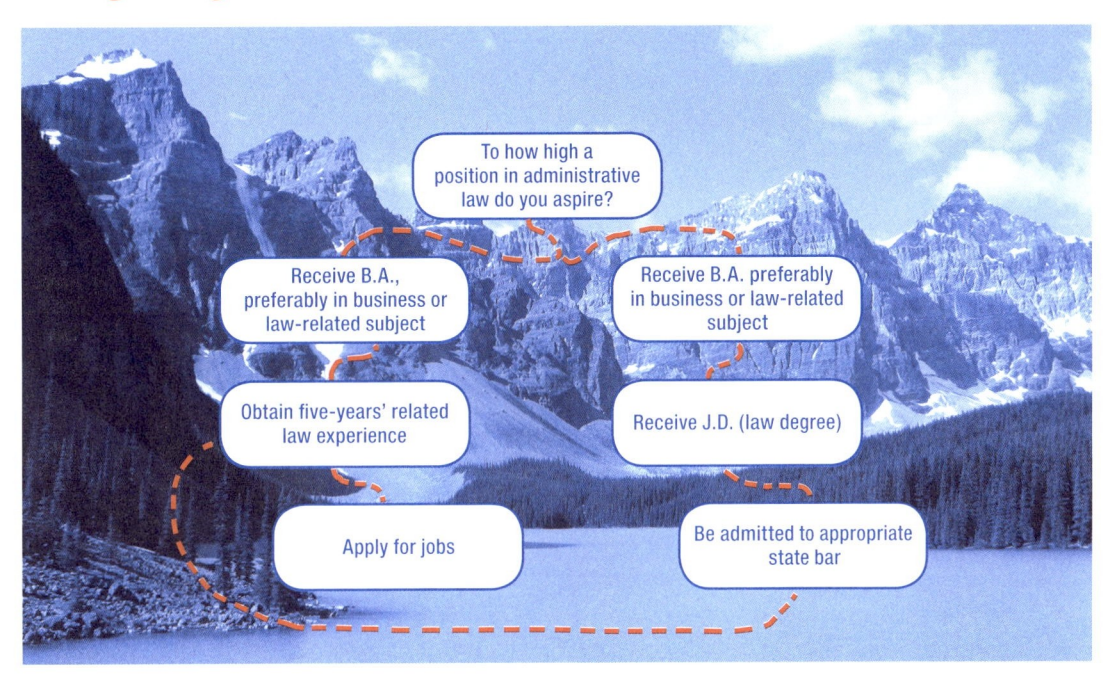

- To how high a position in administrative law do you aspire?
  - Receive B.A., preferably in business or law-related subject
    - Obtain five-years' related law experience
    - Apply for jobs
  - Receive B.A. preferably in business or law-related subject
    - Receive J.D. (law degree)
    - Be admitted to appropriate state bar

transportation and transportation safety, drug enforcement, environment, aviation, mass communications, energy, maritime affairs, mine safety and health, domestic and international trade, food and drugs, and civil service. State-level ALJs, hearing officers, and adjudicators have areas of specialization similar to those at the federal level.

Organizing Your Expedition

Before you commit yourself to this field, assess your goal and area of special interest.

Decide on a destination. Do you want a position that requires only a B.A. plus experience, or do you want a post that requires a law degree plus experience? Jobs requiring a B.A. are not necessarily easier to find in this field, and you may face stiff competition from those who also have law degrees. Nevertheless, there are positions in which your knowledge of a particular area like health, the environment, or commerce is at least

LAW AND JUSTICE

Notes from the Field
Tyrone T. Butler
Administrative law judge
Washington, D.C.

What were you doing before you decided to change careers?

I was raised in a single-parent family in Brooklyn, New York. I joined the NYC Police Department at the age of 21 and retired as a lieutenant after 25 years of service. During that time I'd also graduated from John Jay College of Criminal Justice and received my law degree. After retiring, I took a job as general counsel in the Connecticut Inspector General's office. Then I moved to upstate New York, and found a job nearby as an assistant district attorney in Dutchess County.

Why did you change your career?

There were no prospects for career growth as an assistant district attorney in this area at that time, and salaries were a bare minimum. I

as important as your knowledge of administrative law. Jobs requiring a law degree plus experience, while more prestigious, are also highly competitive, requiring passage of both oral and written exams. Seek advice from individuals in both B.A. and J.D. positions in order to assess where you might best fit in.

Scout the terrain. It may be possible to take a course in administrative law as an unmatriculated student at a local law school to get an overview of the possibilities in this area. You should also take courses in specialties you are considering at both the undergraduate and graduate levels to keep up to speed with the latest developments in these fields. Network on professional networks like LinkedIn to find lawyers in possible specialty areas. Ask them questions about their work. Use the ABA Web site's career counseling feature to communicate with lawyers in the field of administrative law about their specialties.

Find the path that is right for you. Your coursework, Web search, and talks with lawyers in the field should help you in choosing a specialty.

found I could double my salary by becoming an administrative law judge in the New York State Department of Health.

How did you make the transition?

I had put out a lot of résumés. I had interviewed earlier with the New York State Department of Health, but there were no vacancies. This time I was hired. After 2 1/2 years I became the chief administrative law judge of the department. I served in this post for 12 years before moving to Washington to become Chief Administrative Law Judge of the newly established Washington, D.C. Office of Administrative Hearings, where I have served since 2003.

What are the keys to success in your career?

I like what I'm doing. I'm very interested in the process of administrative adjudication. I enjoy the company of my fellow ALJs because we share the same interests. I don't know if I would be as successful if I were, say, a corporation counsel or private attorney doing something for myself. As an administrative law judge, I feel I am giving something back to the public.

So will jobs in the executive departments of government that deal with your specialty, whether it is commerce, agriculture, defense, or one of the many others.

Go back to school. You will need a law degree if you aim for an ALJ post at the federal level or many similar posts at the state and local level. That means three more years of school (not to mention the 5+ years of experience in your specialty field) before you can think about a job in your chosen profession. Having a clear goal through it all, however, should help make your journey worthwhile.

Landmarks

If you are in your twenties . . . Unless you have resources to attend law school full time, now may be the best period in which to develop expertise in your specialty area. If law school is not a current option, then many government departments offer employment that can deepen your specialized knowledge and qualify you for many jobs.

If you are in your thirties or forties . . . If you can now afford law school, part-time jobs in the law and summer internships available to law students will help you strengthen your experience. Even if law school is not a preferred or financially feasible option, the more experience you can gain in your specialty, the more positions that do not require a law degree will become available to you.

If you are in your fifties . . . If your work experiences thus far include enough background in a specialty, then even without a law degree it could be a good time to seek work as an ALJ in that specialty. Nor is it too late—if you have the specialized knowledge, necessary motivation, and desire for a more prestigious position—to go to law school and then seek work as an ALJ.

If you are over sixty . . . The impartiality, independence, personal integrity, and confidentiality that are essential to being a successful ALJ are often the product of experience and maturity as much as one's schooling. It is no accident that many, if not most, judges are found in this age group. If your degree and credentials match a particular job, your age could tip the decision of whom to hire in your favor.

Further Resources

The **National Association of Administrative Law Judiciary (NAALJ),** the largest professional organization of its kind, is a nonprofit corporation whose members include federal, state, and local ALJs, hearing officers, and others in similar positions. The NAALJ Web site contains valuable links to each state's ALJ division and a graphic illustration (and explanation) of which 26 states have a Central Hearing Panel structure that separate the ALJ functions from the executive branch, and which states' executive agencies retain their own ALJs.   http://www.naalj.org

The **National Association of Hearing Officials** has made its goal the improvement of the administrative hearing process. NAHO promotes professionalism in hearing officers and ALJs, provides training and continuing education, and is a national forum for discussion of pertinent issues. NAHO holds an annual conference that is open to anyone interested in the administration hearing process. Downloads from the last conference are available on its Web site.   http://www.naho.org

Legal Assistant (Paralegal)

Legal Assistant (Paralegal)

Career Compasses

Get your bearings on what it takes to be a successful paralegal.

Communication Skills to convey information and elicit understanding (30%)

Relevant Knowledge of the sector(s) of the law for which you are responsible (30%)

Organizational Skills in managing time and workload (20%)

Ability to Manage Stress in dealing with workload and other job issues (20%)

Destination: Legal Assistant (Paralegal)

Behind many a successful lawyer you will find a professional legal assistant, or paralegal. The American Bar Association defines a paralegal as someone "qualified by education, training, or work experience who is employed or retained by a lawyer, law office, corporation, governmental agency, or other entity who performs specifically delegated substantive legal work for which a lawyer is responsible."

LEGAL ASSISTANT (PARALEGAL)

Paralegals interview clients, check the facts of cases, research cases pertinent to a specific legal issue, help prepare legal arguments for trials, update files, and draft documents. Their work may also include drawing up contracts, preparing tax returns, setting up trust funds, and planning estates. Paralegals may not actually practice law—for example, they may not set fees, give legal advice, and present cases in court—but may be authorized to represent clients at administrative hearings.

Paralegals work in many areas of law ranging from corporate to labor to bankruptcy. The smaller the firm the more likely a paralegal is to work in more than one area. In larger firms, by contrast, a paralegal may specialize in one area like intellectual property or labor, or even one aspect of labor law like employee benefits. If you work for a corporation or the government, you will most likely work the usual 40-hour week. If you work for a law firm, however, be prepared to work up to twice that number when the firm is under deadline pressure. Most of the work is done in an office or law library, but occasionally paralegals may have to travel to gather depositions or do other work.

Essential Gear

Take a broad view. Steven W. Schneider's *The Everything Guide to Being a Paralegal* (Adams Media, 2006) covers paralegal career options and legal specialties, with separate chapters on criminal law, product liability, family law, wills and trusts, real property, and contracts. Other sections deal with the specific kinds of tasks that paralegals do, as well as ethics and professional responsibility and the American court and legal systems.

Many paralegals were once trained on the job in much the same way as lawyers: by working for an experienced attorney. Some paralegals are still trained that way. Others without any previous legal training may be hired because they have a background in such fields as tax preparation, criminal justice, consumer affairs, or some aspect of the health industry. Most paralegals today, however, come to the profession by one of two routes. Either they study in a paralegal program at a community college and receive an associate's degree, or they first earn a four-year college degree and then go on to study for a certificate in paralegal studies.

Not surprisingly, the standards in these paralegal programs vary widely, since some take only a few months to complete while others require two years or more. Of the more than 1,000 educational institutions that offer paralegal training, only about 260 meet the approval of the American Bar Association. You can find a list of these programs on the ABA's Web site. Ideally, prospective paralegals should aim for a program that includes internships and job placement services. If possible, interview recent graduates about their experiences in the program before making your choice of programs. Keep in mind that not all employers require graduation from an ABA-approved program, but certificate holders from such programs will most likely have an advantage in the job market.

Once you have graduated from a paralegal training program, several national organizations offer further certification that should be an advantage in the marketplace. For example, the National Association of Legal Assistants (NALA), the largest organization of its kind, offers the Certified Legal Assistant (CLA) or Certified Paralegal (CP) credential. These designations go to those who have passed a two-day examination covering written communications, legal knowledge and skills, ethics and judgment, and all areas of substantive law and who have one of the following qualifications:

> ### Essential Gear
> **Zoom in for some close-ups.** Ursula Furi-Perry's *Fifty Legal Careers for Non-Lawyers* (American Bar Association, 2008) includes 10 careers in growing areas for paralegals, as well as other positions, from entry-level to those with special skills. Includes interviews, bibliography.

1. graduation from a paralegal program that is ABA-approved; or an associate degree program; or a post-baccalaureate certificate program in legal assistant studies; or a B.A. program in legal assistant studies; or a legal assistant program with a minimum of 60 semester hours, of which at least 15 are in substantive legal courses
2. a bachelor's degree in any field plus one year's experience as a paralegal. Fifteen semester hours of substantive legal courses substitute for one year's experience as a paralegal
3. a high school diploma or equivalent plus seven years experience as a paralegal under the supervision of a member of the Bar, plus 20 hours of continuing legal education completed within two years prior to the examination date.

LEGAL ASSISTANT (PARALEGAL)

Similar programs are offered by the National Federation of Paralegal Associations (NFPA) and NALS: the association for legal professionals. An excellent chart comparing the programs and certificates of NFPA, NALA, and NALS is found at http://www.nals.org/certification/comp-chart.html.

Like any profession, paralegals are subject to the effects of the business cycle on their particular specialties. During a recession, for example, demand for paralegals involved in real estate transactions and corporate litigation may decrease, but there is likely to be increased demand for work in bankruptcy, foreclosures, and divorces. A projected growth rate of 22 percent for paralegals to 2016 makes this profession an attractive one indeed for those who have the interest and who meet the requirements.

Navigating the Terrain

- Where are you now? How will you become a paralegal?
- Gain degree and one year's experience
- Serve internship if available
- Take certification exam if needed
- Apply for jobs

You Are Here

Before you begin to explore this career, ask yourself some questions.

Can you relate to a wide variety of people? Paralegals communicate with people from all walks of life. They need keen listening skills in order to get to the heart of what people are really saying. Knowledge of a foreign language, while not required, is also helpful.

Are you computer literate and an excellent writer? Paralegals need word processing skills and the ability to do online legal research in order to assist attorneys. Their writing must also be clear and concise since attorneys will use their findings and reports to prepare legal documents.

Can you work long hours under deadline pressure? Paralegals who work in the private sector must be prepared to work overtime when the project demands it. Paralegals who work for the government, however, work more regular hours.

Organizing Your Expedition

Compare the different routes to meet your goal.

Decide on a destination. An interest in becoming a paralegal could lead to a position in one of several different work environments. Beside traditional law firms, large and small, which employ about 70 percent of all legal assistants, paralegals work in the legal departments of corporations and government offices. Aspiring paralegals should also consider in which area of the law they are especially interested. Large law firms handle all kinds of cases, while smaller ones may specialize in such areas as personal injury, real estate, immigration, or family law. Government lawyers' specialties vary according to the particular department in which they work.

Scout the terrain. Taking a class in legal studies at your local community college or in the continuing education division of a local university can give you a good idea of what a career as a paralegal might involve. Your work experience may also give you a way to segue into a related paralegal career. If your background is in sales or marketing, for example, you might investigate law firms that do work in product liability. If your work in manufacturing or construction has led to an interest in labor law, check out government departments and law firms that focus on that area. Or you might seek a temporary position in a law firm where you can use your word processing and computer skills to learn how contracts are constructed and worded. The possibilities are many, and it is up to you to connect the dots that could lead to a position in your preferred field.

Find the path that is right for you. Do you have a clear idea in which work environment and/or specialty you want to end up? Then you may find that your best bet is to investigate paralegal programs that are either stand-alone or part of a local community college. On the other hand, if your career focus is less defined, you may want to seek temporary positions at law firms or with lawyers in individual or small group practices where you can gain hands-on experience that will give you a clearer idea of what sort of paralegal career is best suited to you.

Landmarks

If you are in your twenties . . . As a recent graduate of either high school or college you may find it easier than an older person to return to the classroom for either a certificate course or a two-year degree course in paralegal studies.

If you are in your thirties or forties . . . If you are motivated, a paralegal studies program can help redirect your work experience from another area like sales, manufacturing, or administration into a new career as a legal assistant.

If you are in your fifties . . . Persons with the drive and stamina to obtain their paralegal certificate and then to work the sometimes long hours required of a paralegal may find that their previous work experience and judgment will give them an edge when applying for jobs in as a legal assistant.

LAW AND JUSTICE

Notes from the Field
Linda J. Wolf
Advanced certified paralegal
Dallas, Texas

What were you doing before you decided to change careers?

I received a journalism scholarship for college and worked for a regional newspaper while I was in college. I planned to continue my career in journalism.

Why did you change your career?

I was disappointed at the starting pay scale for print reporters, so I considered going to law school. However, I needed something more flexible because my parents had been advised they might be shipped overseas, which would have left me responsible for my younger sister. I also didn't want to take on the financial burden of law school. While I contemplated my choices, a college friend suggested a paralegal career that would be more flexible and much less expensive.

How did you make the transition?

Journalism is an excellent portal into legal work, because of the strong emphasis on communication and research. I also loved science and had started college as a physics major but changed to a double major in

If you are over sixty . . . Older individuals with the perseverance to take legal studies courses during these economically troubled times may actually find a pleasant surprise in store when they seek work. There is often more work for paralegals, older and otherwise, during recessions. In fact, the job category of paralegals, in which people generally make less money than attorneys, was first recognized by the American Bar Association in 1968 as a way for law firms to cut costs during economic downturns.

Further Resources

NALS This national association for legal professionals was formerly limited in membership to legal secretaries but now also includes paralegals journalism and political science, because I wasn't sure what I would do with physics when I graduated. I interviewed at a law firm that specialized in intellectual property. They wanted someone with strong editing skills, which I possessed. As it turned out, my science courses also gave me a leg up. I was hired and have been with the same group of lawyers for nearly 29 years.

In the firm, paralegals are assigned to individual partners, and I was fortunate enough to work with a partner who was a chemical engineer. He encouraged me to augment my education with chemistry courses to help me understand the cases we worked on. He was my supervising attorney and mentor until his retirement.

What are the keys to success in your career?

Stay engaged. There is always something new to learn. Some paralegals assume that once they obtain their degree or certificate and find a job that they've made it, but that's only the start. It's important to pursue credentials of excellence, like the Certified Paralegal and Advanced Certified Paralegal designations, and then stay on top of the trends and changes in the law through continuing legal education. We also need to market ourselves to our employers. Paralegals can't sit back in their offices and wait for the work to come to them. We have to demonstrate that we are honing our skills and are capable of tackling new challenges.

and legal assistants. Its Web site includes a chart comparing basic information about NALA, NALS, and NFPA (National Federation of Paralegal Associations); and a career center and an online learning center and online study group sessions. In the learning center, members can take courses in the skills tested for three certificates: the ALS (Accredited Legal Secretary), PLS (Professional in Legal Services), and PP (Professional Paralegal).   http://www.nals.org

The National Association of Legal Assistants is the largest organization representing paralegals in the United States. Under the heading "About Paralegals" on its Web site, you will find a discussion of the definition of *paralegal*; NALA's current model standards and guidelines for utilizing paralegals; details of two recent Supreme Court cases that ruled in favor of paralegal fee reimbursement; and extensive advice on evaluating paralegal education programs. The Web site also features links to 35 state-level paralegal associations.   http://www.nala.org

Paralegal Assistant Today magazine has a Web site that includes hundreds of related articles, arranged by subject, on topics of interest to the profession. The Web site also includes e-mail lists open to all and a special section called Students/Education.   http://www.legalassistant.com/profession

Legal Secretary

Legal Secretary

Career Compasses

Get up to speed in developing the skills you will need as a legal secretary.

Communication Skills to clarify instructions and keep your office running smoothly (30%)

Organizational Skills to assign priorities and manage workflow (25%)

Ability to Manage Stress in order to avoid work fatigue and assure high productivity (25%)

Relevant Knowledge of legal terminology and document formats (20%)

Destination: Legal Secretary

Every profession has its own language, and legal secretaries are fluent in the language of the law. For them, *garnish* is not something you put on a salad, nor does *lien* describe the amount of fat in a cut of meat. Legal secretaries' knowledge of legal language, ability to take dictation, and expertise in producing basic legal documents, among many other skills, has made their occupation a key part of the world of the law. Legal secretaries also organize documents and case files, schedule conferences and maintain attorney calendars, use services like Lexis and Westlaw to find court decisions pertinent to the case at hand, and take notes at meetings, hearings, and depositions.

Legal secretaries acquire their skills by two main routes. It is possible to become a legal secretary either by obtaining a high school education that emphasizes office skills, or by enrolling in a one- or two-year program in office administration at a business or technical school or community college. Some jobs as legal secretary require a bachelor's degree. Legal secretaries should also have some knowledge of laws, court procedures, government regulations, and other factors that affect legal practice. Once on the job, most legal secretaries get additional training in-house. Some take outside classes to keep up with new office technologies.

Like all secretaries, legal secretaries must be competent in typing, spelling, grammar, punctuation, and speaking. They must get along well with people, since they may be dealing not only with other staff but also with clients. Legal secretaries, especially those in higher-level positions, must exercise tact and common sense in making judgments, and be able to work independently.

Essential Gear

Hit the books. For example, *Basic Manual for the Lawyer's Assistant*, 9th ed. (Thomsen West, 2007). Used by NALS in its ALS and PLS exam preparation, this text deals with every aspect of the legal secretary's job, including ethics, the law office, computers, accounting, oral and written communications, preparation of legal documents, and the various types of law.

There is no telling where the skills acquired by study and work in a law firm may take you in life. Erin Brockovich was working as a receptionist in the California law firm of Masry & Vititoe when her boss asked her to do some research on a water pollution case involving a large company. Finding some suspicious blood samples in the company files, Brockovich ended up helping Masry & Vititoe win a $333 million settlement for the plaintiffs and receiving a personal bonus of $2.5 million for her work. Her story is the basis of the feature film *Erin Brockovich* (2000), starring Julia Roberts. Today Erin Brockovich heads her own consulting firm dealing with environmental issues.

Erin Brockovich is not a typical case, of course, but any ambitious legal secretary can draw a valuable lesson from the story: Never turn down an opportunity to expand your range of skills by taking on a new and challenging task. This lesson holds true whether you are seeking a temporary sales job that will hone your interpersonal abilities or studying for a certificate that formally measures your secretarial skills.

After taking a one- or two-year course in legal education like those already described, or acquiring experience working in a law office, budding legal secretaries may sit for a certificate exam such as the ALS (Accredited Legal Secretary), offered by NALS. The ALS exam takes four hours and has three parts: Written Communications; Office Procedures and Legal Knowledge; and Ethics, Human Relations, and Judgment. Having an ALS certification shows potential employers that you are serious about your dedication to this occupation. Students can prepare for the certificate exam by reading materials available from the NALS bookstore and participating in online study group sessions that are free and generally open to the public. Sessions are listed by date and time at http://www.nals.org/onlinelearning/index.html.

> ## Essential Gear
> **Hunt for jobs.** Legal Secretaries International's Legal Career Center Network has links to over 90 online career centers on more than 90 state and local bar association Web sites, more than 20 paralegal/legal secretary associations, and many major related Web portals. You can search for jobs by type, location, type of law practice, and key words for part of the United States. http://lsintl.legalstaff.com

Your education as a legal secretary will continue even after you are hired, since office technologies, including updated software packages and information storage systems, continue to evolve, thus requiring in-service training. Similarly, as your legal skills increase, you may want to sit for advanced certification exams such as the PLS (Professional Legal Secretary) offered by NALS or the CLSS (Certified Legal Secretary Specialist) offered by Legal Secretaries International in six specialized fields: Business Law, Civil Litigation, Criminal Law, Intellectual Property, Probate, and Real Estate.

It cannot be said too often how legal training at any level can be a stepping-stone to a job in a related field. Just as lawyers often go on to related occupations in business, government, and the nonprofit sector, legal secretaries may advance to many other jobs, including executive secretary, office manager, supervisor of word processing, software instructor or sales representative, or paralegal. Work hard and the choice is yours.

LEGAL SECRETARY

You Are Here

Focus your job search by considering a few questions.

Do I like activities where I must follow fixed rules and routines? You will have plenty of opportunity to show initiative as a legal secretary. Most of the time, however, you will be working with somebody else's ideas, not your own. Your concern is more with getting the facts and details right in what others are saying. Your boss, not your brain, is often your final authority when you have a question.

Do I have an enterprising spirit? A legal secretary with experience may be given projects that involve leading other people and making decisions. These decisions are often business-related and may involve risk taking. If you are looking to grow in your position and take on more responsibilities, a "yes" answer to this question may open the door to advancement.

Navigating the Terrain

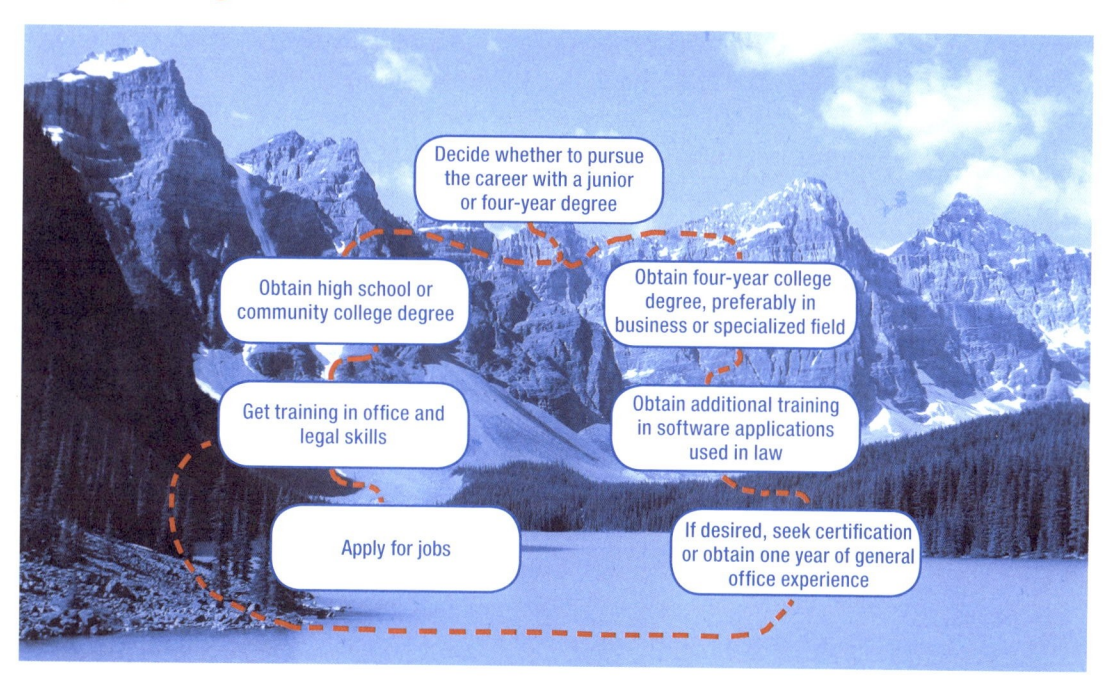

- Decide whether to pursue the career with a junior or four-year degree
- Obtain high school or community college degree
- Obtain four-year college degree, preferably in business or specialized field
- Get training in office and legal skills
- Obtain additional training in software applications used in law
- Apply for jobs
- If desired, seek certification or obtain one year of general office experience

Notes from the Field

Karen L. Hudson
Legal secretary
Washington, D.C.

What were you doing before you decided to change careers?

I got married right after high school and didn't get to start college. Before I changed careers I was a word processor. I advanced as far as I could go to being the supervisor, then became an independent contractor.

Why did you change your career?

I was bored and didn't see where else I could go, except to carpal tunnel syndrome with all the typing. I went out on maternity leave to have my second child and decided that I needed to do something else. I wanted a career so I tried to think of something I was really interested in and came up with the law.

Am I an organized person who can multitask? Legal secretaries not only perform traditional tasks like recording, storing, and retrieving information—they often also take on certain managerial tasks like planning and scheduling meetings and managing projects. Legal secretaries must prioritize all their jobs in order to keep the workflow in the office moving at an efficient pace.

Organizing Your Expedition

Before you determine your direction, scope out the field.

Decide on a destination. Your decision to become a legal secretary in one sense narrows the field for your expedition, since legal secretaries make up only 12 percent of all specialized secretaries (including executive secretaries, administrative assistants, and medical secretaries). In another sense, however, the number of potential employers remains large, since they include not only law firms and corporation law departments, but government agencies, nonprofits, and solo practices.

LEGAL SECRETARY

How did you make the transition?

I was too old for law school so I settled on becoming a paralegal. After getting my paralegal certificate I could not get a job, because I had been typing forever, but not in a law firm. One of my classmates from the paralegal school called me about an interview he had just come from close to my home. He didn't type very well and didn't get the job. He knew I typed 90 words per minute and had recommended me. He said they were waiting for me to call. I interviewed and was hired and started that same day. I became the paralegal/secretary for a small family law firm that specialized in criminal, bankruptcy, personal injury, and real estate law.

What are the keys to your success in your career?

I would say the keys to success in my career are: Performing all tasks with a smile, asking if I don't understand, being a team player, always conducting myself in a professional manner, and continuing my legal education to stay current.

The trick is to figure out which organizations are most likely to hire you. For example, during recessions, firms that specialize in bankruptcies, foreclosures, and divorces are more in demand than those handling real estate and estate planning. Bone up on the law specialties that are now hot in your geographic area and plan your search accordingly. Do not neglect your particular personal passions, whether they are health issues, education, or some other issue. List the public agencies and private companies that deal with the law in those areas.

Scout the terrain. Go down your list of organizations and inquire via Web site, phone, or letter about openings for legal secretaries. Keep a log of your inquiries and follow up those leads that look promising. When speaking about a job opening, emphasize your personal interest, qualifications, and experience in the field. Remember that persistence can be a positive sign of your desire for the job as long as your approach is assertive but aggressive in nature. Remember, your employer is looking for someone who has an enterprising spirit but is also a team player.

Find the path that is right for you. If there are jobs available for which you are qualified, and you have followed the preceding steps diligently and persistently, you should eventually find your way to a job that could be the first building block in a career with many prospects and possibilities. Your transition from job hunter to job holder should be all the smoother for one reason: the very enterprising spirit and willingness to follow prescribed procedures that made you a successful job hunter are also two key qualities in a successful legal secretary.

Landmarks

If you are in your twenties . . . As a recent high school or college graduate, your decision to add office experience or specialized legal training to become a legal secretary could give you a head start over those whose career plans are more unfocused.

If you are in your thirties or forties . . . If you now have both academic and real-world office experience under your belt, you can bring a more knowledgeable perspective to a one- or two-year program to prepare you to become a legal secretary.

If you are in your fifties . . . Your work experience in a law-related field like medicine and health care, insurance, business, or the environment, among others, will have more personal meaning when you train to become a legal secretary.

If you are over sixty . . . If your eyesight and typing speed still meet job requirements, your greater maturity and experience in making judgments and decisions will give you a real advantage as you train for this job.

Further Resources

NALS The association for legal professionals is well known for its ALS and PLS certification levels and the training classes that it offers, both online and in classrooms in many states, to prepare candidates for careers as legal secretaries and other legal services support staff.
http://www.nals.org

LEGAL SECRETARY

Mary A. DeVries, ***The Legal Secretary's Complete Handbook, 4th ed.*** (Prentice Hall, 1992). This comprehensive work covers the legal secretary's general duties as well as sections on preparing legal instruments and documents, preparing court papers, specialized practices, and legal facts and secretarial aids.

Court Officer (Bailiff)

Court Officer (Bailiff)

Career Compasses

Master the skills one must balance to become an effective court officer or bailiff.

Caring about your commitment to enforce laws and protect people (25%)

Communication Skills to convey directions and elicit others' cooperation (25%)

Relevant Knowledge of the specific laws and procedures that apply to your cases as well as their larger context (25%)

Ability to Manage Stress in dealing with hostile parties inside and outside court (25%)

Destination: Court Officer (Bailiff)

We have all seen those TV legal dramas where someone noisily interrupts the courtroom proceedings. The judge bangs his gavel and orders the offending party to be removed. Court officers are the persons who carry out the judge's orders. Court officers are also known in different jurisdictions as bailiffs, sheriff's deputies, marshals, or constables, particularly when they work outside as well as inside the courthouse. Working efficiently and quietly but forcefully, court officers help assure the smooth running of the court system. They guard defendants on the way to and from the courtroom to make sure they do not escape; monitor the jury when it is sequestered to make sure it has no outside contact; and in general enforce courtroom decorum. Court officers also assist the judge by swearing in witnesses, passing documents from party to party, and keeping trials moving forward efficiently. In some states and jurisdictions, the court officer may also serve and enforce summonses, subpoenas, and arrest warrants, and seize contraband. In other jurisdictions, the court officer works exclusively within the court system.

The word *bailiff* comes from the Anglo-French word *bail*, which meant "custody." The word originally came from the Latin *bajulare*, "to carry a burden" or "support." Both the Anglo-French and Latin meanings have carried over in the present sense of the word: to exert authority in maintaining order in the court, and to support judges by carrying out their orders. By the way, bailiffs have nothing directly to do with the collection or processing of bail, which is the money that a judge may require defendants to put up in order to leave prison and assure their appearance in court.

> ## *Essential Gear*
> **This could be your life.** A seven-and-a-half minute video, "Be a New York State Court Officer," though a bit long on testimonials, depicts well the everyday life of a court officer in the unified court system in New York State. http://www.nycourts.gov/careers/coexams.shtml

In 2006, court officers made up only 19,000 of the 500,000 correctional officers counted by the Bureau of Labor Statistics as employed. The larger category also includes those responsible for overseeing prison and jail inmates. Court officers' salaries are slightly lower than those of correctional officers, but their hours are much more regular than those of others in the larger category, and working conditions are much less stressful. Like correctional officers, the majority of all court officers work at the state and local level. Attracted by the opportunity to have a secure career with regular hours and be able to raise a family, women make up as many as 25 percent of court officers in some jurisdictions.

To be hired as a court officer at all levels of the court system, you must be a U.S. citizen or permanent resident and have no felony convictions. You must be physically fit and have good eyesight and hearing. Candidates must be screened for drug abuse, undergo a background check by the FBI, and pass a written examination. Some state and local positions

COURT OFFICER (BAILIFF)

require either some college or law enforcement or military experience. In practice, half of all correction officers today have an associate's or a bachelor's degree. Some courts require two years of previous work experience, not necessarily related to corrections or law enforcement, as evidence of job stability.

Requirements for becoming a court officer depend partly on which level of court—county, state, or federal—you are aiming at. It is possible to become a court officer in smaller jurisdictions with as little as a high school education and some formal training. The local courthouse where you live can tell you the requirements for court officers in your area. Court officers in larger jurisdictions with more specialized functions may need a bachelor's degree and more training.

> ### Essential Gear
> **Win through words.** *Verbal Judo: The Gentle Art of Persuasion*, by George Thompson and Jerry B. Jenkins (HarperCollins, 2004), describes and illustrates a method of using empathy, active listening, and other strategies to communicate your point of view in disputes and thereby gain the upper hand. Thompson has a teaching and law enforcement background.

This training takes place at regional academies that have been set up under professional correctional association guidelines. Training course curricula vary by state, but in general candidates receive instruction in firearms, first aid/CPR, and custody and security procedures. Following academic instruction, candidates undergo on-the-job training that may last for several weeks or months.

The most selective standards for court officers are those in federal courts, which require all entry-level applicants to have a bachelor's degree; three years of experience in counseling, assisting, or supervising individuals; or a combination of higher education plus related experience totaling seven years.

No matter how high you are aiming in your court career, the aspiring court officer should have a basic dedication to the principles of justice and the law and treat individuals fairly and in a dignified manner. Court officers must be able to communicate with a wide variety of different people and to elicit their cooperation to ensure the smooth running of the court system. Court officers must have a firm knowledge of court procedures and the ability to carry them out in an efficient manner. Finally, ideal court officers should be able to manage the inevitable stresses of the job without letting them interfere with their work.

Successful court officers have the satisfaction of knowing that they are integral parts of a court system designed to preserve the vital provisions of the Sixth and Seventh Amendments to the U.S. Constitution: "the right to a speedy and public trial, by an impartial jury" and "the right of trial by jury."

You Are Here

Your path to becoming a court officer begins with your basic respect for our legal system.

Do you understand the importance of the American legal system, with its balance of the rights of the individual and those of the state? As a court officer you most protect the rights of individuals in the courtroom as well as assure the smooth functioning of the legal process. You will need personal and organizational skills to assure the cooperation of the various parties and the efficient running of a trial.

Navigating the Terrain

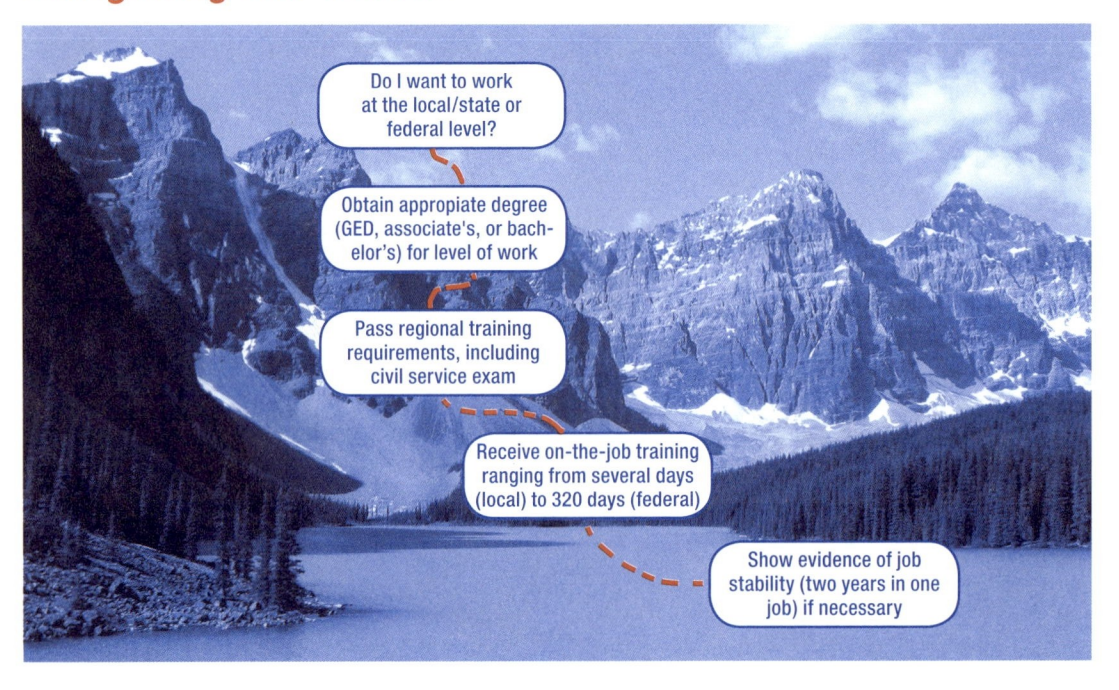

- Do I want to work at the local/state or federal level?
- Obtain appropiate degree (GED, associate's, or bachelor's) for level of work
- Pass regional training requirements, including civil service exam
- Receive on-the-job training ranging from several days (local) to 320 days (federal)
- Show evidence of job stability (two years in one job) if necessary

Can you display both quiet authority and, when necessary, use physical force? The tone of most trials is deliberative and low-key, thanks in part to the court officer's presence, but emotions can sometimes flare. The court officer must be able to respond quickly when an unruly witness, defendant, or spectator disrupts the courtroom.

Can you manage the stress involved in dealing with uncooperative individuals? Court officers accompany criminal defendants to the courtroom. They also assist the judge in maintaining order in a court that often contains individuals who do not like each other very much. Court officers must be able to manage the stress caused in such situations so that it does not affect their work adversely.

Organizing Your Expedition

Before you set out, consider all the possible routes you can take.

Decide on a destination. Determine whether you would feel more comfortable working in a local, state, or federal court system. You should also decide whether you want to work in a jurisdiction where court officers work only in the court system or if you want to combine courtroom duties and local law enforcement work. Consider that local courts usually have the easiest entrance requirements and federal courts the hardest, and standards and working conditions can vary widely from place to place. Inquire at your local court about the requirements for that system. If you want to work in a geographic area with one or more state courts, investigate the state court system as well.

Scout the terrain. Ask court officers at the local, state, or federal level about their jobs. Observe a trial and take careful notice of the role the court officer plays. Question court officers who sometimes work outside the courtroom to serve warrants or to seize or sell property. If their specific assignment does not involve physical danger, you may be able to arrange to accompany bailiffs working outside the courtroom as they go about their daily rounds. Study up for and take the appropriate civil service exam for court officers in your jurisdiction. The exam is in multiple-choice format and is usually three hours long. It tests for clerical

Notes from the Field

Martin Mulholland
Court officer
Central Islip, New York

What were you doing before you decided to change careers?

I was doing route sales for Snyder's and Hanover Pretzels. I had worked in a deli when I was in high school, and I saw that people who worked the routes were home by 3 P.M, so that was a big attraction. I did route sales for 18 years. I also developed new routes and then sold them off to others.

Why did you change your career?

I was a successful route sales operator, but there was not much camaraderie on the job. As an independent operator going in and out of stores, I had little interaction with other route operators, though I enjoyed helping customers. I had played soccer and lacrosse in school and enjoyed being part of a team. I missed having a team spirit in my job. I wanted to be part of something bigger. I have a brother-in-law who is a court officer, and my brother is a firefighter. I saw how strong a bond my

skills, observation and memory, reading comprehension, and related subject matter.

Find the path that is right for you. You may find that you enjoy working in a smaller system where employees are more likely to know each other than in a larger court system. Or you may prefer the higher pay scale and greater sense of professionalism that is more likely to be found in the higher courts. Your chances of being selected are also affected by your exam scores and the number of courts that are hiring. Consider that at the federal level there are only 92 courts: at least one in every state plus Puerto Rico and Washington, D.C., and as many as four in states with larger populations like New York and California. At the state level there are hundreds, if not thousands, of courts. By weighing your abilities and interests as well as the job situation in the geographic area in which you wish to work, you will eventually find the job that is best for you.

brother had with his fellow firefighters, especially after 9/11, when his fire company lost 10 of its members. In talking with my wife, I realized I wanted a job like theirs.

How did you make the transition?

I took the test for court officer and did really well on it. It took a long time to get the results, but when I got them, it just seemed the right move to make. My sales background and life experience gave me the people skills needed. I took a three-month course at the New York State Court Officer's Academy before accepting a position in the New York State Unified Court System on Long Island.

What are the keys to success in your career?

In my three years on the job, I have been able to remain calm on a daily basis even though I work in a criminal court where many of the people, whether victims or defendants, are upset. My training, official appearance, and unthreatening manner are a large reason I succeed in my job. For me, being a court officer has been a life-changing experience. I enjoy working with my fellow court officers and other court personnel, some of whom are now among my closest friends.

Landmarks

If you are in your twenties . . . As a young person you can take advantage of your statistically superior physical fitness to do well on the physical tests usually required of a court officer. Combined with training to develop your judgment and ability to think quickly, your youth can be a distinct advantage when applying to join the judicial system. Candidates in this age group are also more likely to be able to relocate in order to take an available job.

If you are in your thirties or forties . . . Persons in this age group who want to work as court officers are in a better position to meet both the physical and educational requirements than younger candidates. They are more likely to have completed higher education, yet young enough to have fewer problems with the physical tests than older candidates might have.

If you are in your fifties . . . Your education and work experience will both work in your favor as an older person, since applicants in this age group are more likely to have stable work experience than younger candidates, as well as more higher education.

If you are over sixty . . . As long as you remain physically fit and fulfill the educational and other requirements of the job in your particular jurisdiction, your greater maturity and authority as an older person can be a distinct advantage in handling confrontations with unruly defendants and courtroom spectators.

Further Resources

The **National Sheriff's Association** now incorporates the **Court Officers and Deputies Association.** Clicking on the NSA Web site home page under "Court Security" and "Programs and Training," respectively, will take you to an article on court security and information on educational opportunities.   http://www.sheriffs.org

Some state bailiffs and/or court officer associations have their own Web sites. For example, see the **Ohio Bailiffs and Court Officers Association.** Note its code of ethics. Press *News* for articles on recent situations faced by the state bailiffs and court officers.   http://www.ohiobailiffs.com

Court Clerk

Court Clerk

Career Compasses

Of the skills and abilities needed by a court clerk, here are the ones often considered most important.

Relevant Knowledge of the sector of the legal process for which you are responsible (35%)

Communication Skills to convey information and elicit understanding (30%)

Organizational Skills in categorizing, filing, and recalling cases that you handle (20%)

Ability to Manage Stress in dealing with the heavy workload and other job issues (15%)

Destination: Court Clerk

If the main focus of the court officer is maintaining order in the court, the principal task of the court clerk is to maintain the written records of the court. To carry out this task, court clerks perform a wide variety of tasks that vary considerably in scope from state to state and from county to county.

49
COURT CLERK

The basic duties of court clerks may include any or all of the following:

- preparing the list of cases to be called before the court on a given day
- preparing case files and keeping records of the dispositions of cases
- responding to requests for documents or information
- preparing draft agendas or bylaws for town or city council meetings
- answering official correspondence and maintaining fiscal records
- issuing licenses or permits, administering tests, and collecting fees

Court clerks have different names in different jurisdictions. In Oregon, for example, court clerks are called judicial services specialists. Nationally, almost seven out of 10 court clerks in a given state work at the local level, while the rest work at the state level. This ratio, however, does not apply to every state, nor does it necessarily suggest the number of job openings in a given state. Most job openings are in state court systems.

Essential Gear

Court Clerks Central. In addition to being a font of information about state courts in general, the Web site of the National Center for State Courts has job listings for all levels of state court clerks from chief deputy court clerk to courtroom clerk, with full descriptions of duties. http://www.ncsconline.org/D_KIS/jobdeda/Jobs_Clerks(8).htm

For court clerks with limited duties, the job requirements are often a high school diploma plus short-term on-the-job training, although sometimes two years of college or business school may be required. For court clerk jobs with more responsibilities, bachelor's degrees are preferred. Some court clerks at the federal level also have law degrees or master's degrees, and all are appointed to office. Court clerks are not to be confused with a position that is usually called clerk of the court. This is an administrative post often filled through election. In Virginia, for example, the Clerk of the Circuit Court is elected to an eight-year term and has over 800 responsibilities. Nor should court clerks be confused with law clerks, who have law degrees and are selected (usually from a long list of applicants) by the judges for whom they will work.

Duties of court clerks vary by jurisdiction, but most require a number of skills that may include word processing, bookkeeping, accounting, and budgeting. In addition, they may need written and spoken English skills—

even fluency in a second language in some areas of the United States—and the ability to read for details and recognize errors in numbers, spelling, and punctuation in written documents. Above all, court clerks need to be able to give and receive instructions calmly and clearly. They must also be able to deal with the stress that may come handling a heavy workload in which there is little room for error and in which the people you work with are also often under stress. Finally, the ideal court clerk has excellent judgment skills, a sense of discretion, and overall integrity.

The typical day of a town court clerk might begin with providing instructions to a visitor about forms to initiate divorce proceedings. Indeed, in over half of divorce and custody cases in many jurisdictions, one or both parties represent themselves and are therefore more likely to require assistance from court staff. On days (or nights) when court is in session, the court clerk prepares the docket of cases, swears in any jurors or witnesses, collects fines, and writes up the results of each case. Cases may involve everything from traffic tickets to robbery, drug and sex crimes, with evictions and foreclosures among the more common cases during recessions. Twice a year court clerks in New York are required to attend a training session to bring them up to date on the latest changes in court procedures.

> ## Essential Gear
> **Make the courts work.** Although intended primarily for teachers and planners, the Web site of the National Association for Court Management Web site has thoughtful information on shortcomings in the current system and ways to improve our courts. http://www.nacmnet.org

Court clerks usually work a five-day, 40-hour week, but their hours may vary according to state and local laws or the orders of judges or others with the power to regulate their hours of work. Court clerks spend most of their time in offices and courtrooms. They may start in a lower position, such as typist, file clerk, and assistant court clerk and advance with experience. Or they may take a civil service exam and score well enough to begin on a higher rung of the career ladder.

Court clerks may fill a slot in a small town court or a county or state-level position with more responsibilities. At each level, by maintaining court dockets and carefully checking and filing documents, court clerks play a key role in carrying out the requirements set forth in Article III of the U.S. Constitution and Amendments VI–VII.

You Are Here

Your journey to becoming a court clerk begins with your respect for the judicial branch.

Do you understand the key role that the court clerk plays in the judicial process? As a court clerk, you document the records of the court accurately so they reflect its proceedings and are available for future reference. Without these records, the court cannot really be said to fully exist.

Can you observe high standards of conduct so that the integrity, impartiality, and independence of the judiciary are preserved? Court clerks, whether at the lowest or highest levels, should behave in a professional manner in order to avoid impropriety or the appearance of impropriety in all activities both inside and outside the courtroom, including family, social, and other relationships.

Navigating the Terrain

- Where are you now? How will you attain a position as a court clerk?
- Earn high school diploma
- Obtain experience at a lower level or in related field
- Earn associate or bachelor's degree as required
- Pass competitive exam if required and apply for jobs

LAW AND JUSTICE

Notes from the Field
Khoben Crossley
Court clerk
Salem, Oregon

What were you doing before you decided to change careers?
> I worked as a treatment counselor, mostly at a residential facility for adolescent girls with emotional and behavioral problems. A typical day in this job involved a great deal of conflict resolution and required effective listening and communication skills.

Why did you change your career?
> I changed career paths due to the inherent level of stress within this type of work. Lack of sleep, a meager paycheck, an overall feeling of defeat over not being able to save everyone, and the expiration of the grace period for repaying my student loans also motivated me to look elsewhere for work. Having graduated with a degree in criminal justice, I applied for a job as a Judicial Specialist II for the Court of Appeals of the State of Oregon. The job description noted among its requirements an ability to remain calm in dealing with hostile people, with which I had plenty of experience.

How did you make the transition?
> I quickly found that I was well suited for the job. I have a studious and voracious work ethic that helps me to keep pace with the workload

Are you an organized person who can keep track of a variety of court records? These may include some or all of the following: marriage licenses, adoption records and guardianships, name changes, liens, judgments and land records, fines, fee payments, and payments in connection with court judgments.

Organizing Your Expedition

Before you set out, consider at what level you wish to work and how specialized you want to be.

Decide on a destination. Consider whether your skills and needs will best fit the requirements of a court clerk at the local level or at a state and ever-changing court procedures and rules. The stress in this job, unlike my previous job, comes from the technical nature of the law itself and the volume of work. Clerks must be able to multitask effectively and to know that they will never see that bottom of their inbox.

What are the keys to success in your career?

Success in this career requires a strong work ethic and effective social skills. My success thus far at the Court of Appeals is directly attributable to my love of learning, ambition, and an ability to communicate with a wide variety of people.

Processing legal documents is a tedious process, and the volume of work is enough to keep each clerk busy full time. However, we also assist the public, whether by phone, e-mail, or in person, and this can take up most of a clerk's day. Although we are prohibited from giving legal advice, we can explain court process and procedures and answer other case-specific questions. We often deal with people who are very angry and frustrated with the technical, legal nature of the court process. A clerk must remain calm and give appropriate, accurate information.

A career within the judicial department is exciting. It is fast paced and challenging and offers a wide range of opportunities.

level. Keep in mind that court duties, standards, and working conditions can vary widely depending on the court's location and jurisdiction. Some court clerks mainly handle documents; others must deal with the public as well. The degree of specialization can vary depending on the size of the jurisdiction. The best way to begin to find out which judicial environment is most compatible with your interests and abilities is to inquire at the court or courts that serve your area, or check the state Web sites that serve your area. To find your state and local court Web sites, go to http://www.ncsconline.org/D_kis/info_court_web_sites.html. Click on "State Court Web sites" (which also includes local and municipal courts), and explore the different choices within the geographic area in which you want to work.

Scout the terrain. Prepare a list of questions you would like to ask court clerks with different levels of responsibility. Focus not only on their basic duties, but also on how they got their jobs (including how they transitioned from their previous jobs), what they like and dislike about their positions, and what enables them to succeed in their work. Then establish contact either through a visit to a courthouse or by telephone and e-mail contact with a court official who handles public relations. You can also find out much about court clerks by surfing the Web sites referred to in the section above, especially for any job postings that describe the duties and salary of the position. For example, go to http://www.ncsconline.org and click on "Job Descriptions."

Find the path that is right for you. Having carefully surveyed the position of court clerk at various levels and interviewed one or more court clerks, you should be in a much better position to decide upon the career path that is best for you. Taking a civil service test for court clerk after self-study or a short-term course may also help you decide if you have the aptitude to apply for a higher-level post. A position in a town or small city may offer less prestige or salary than a position in the state capital or in the higher courts. Yet your comfort level and clear-headed assessment of your own talents and skills must also play an important part in your decision.

Landmarks

If you are in your twenties . . . The energy and enthusiasm in this age group can go a long way toward making up for any lack of experience at this early stage of one's career. The stamina and a drive often found in twentysomethings can be a real plus when tackling the overflowing in-boxes and meeting the quick turn-around times that many court clerks face.

If you are in your thirties or forties . . . If you have skills in word processing, bookkeeping, or other office skills, your experience, when added to your greater maturity, can make your résumé stand out when applying for court clerk jobs.

If you are in your fifties . . . The efficient work habits and communication skills that persons in this age group have learned through experience can give them an advantage in handling this demanding, multitasking job.

If you are over sixty . . . The varied work and life experiences of those in this age group can be a real plus in relating to the varied situations presented by members of the public who seek the help of court clerks.

Further Resources

The **Federal Court Clerk Association (FCCA)** was formed in 1922 to "promote the professionalism and integrity of the federal judiciary . . . to support the independence of the judiciary, and to foster cooperation between the courts and the community" through annual conferences and award programs. Members come from the district courts, circuit courts, bankruptcy court, "probation employees, court reporters, and other stakeholders in the federal court system." This Web site contains valuable links to all state court Web sites. http://www.fcca.ws/links.htm

Court Reporter

Court Reporter

Career Compasses

Keep up the pace by knowing the characteristics of a successful court reporter.

Organizational Skills to manage a large volume of recordings and transcripts (30%)

Ability to Manage Stress involved in maintaining exacting schedules and producing speedy and accurate records of what you are recording and transcribing (25%)

Relevant Knowledge of the special terms used in your particular venue (20%)

Communication Skills to clarify the meaning of what you hear (25%)

Destination: Court Reporter

Those who can take dictation or transcribe documents have long had a respected place in society, beginning in the Middle Ages with the clerks (a word with the same root as *cleric*) who painstakingly transcribed and preserved Holy Scripture. Today the dictation and transcription process is much faster, to say the least! Experienced courtroom stenographers, for example, can take down trial proceedings at more than 225 words per minute by pressing multiple keys at once on a stenotype machine and creating abbreviations that represent sounds, words, and phrases. These abbreviations are then translated and displayed as text by a process known as computer-aided transcription.

Other methods of court reporting include electronic reporting. Here the court reporter monitors the audio recording of a court session, taking notes to identify speakers. The reporter is then often responsible for making a written transcript of the recording. In a third method of court reporting called *voice writing*, the court reporter repeats everything said in court into a special microphone that is masked by a voice silencer. The silencer prevents the reporter's voice from being heard in the courtroom. Some voice writers create a real-time transcript by using speech-recognition technology. Others later transcribe everything they recorded into written words, either with speech recognition technology or by manually typing the transcript.

In addition to transcribing court sessions, court reporters must edit their transcripts in order to correct the grammar and spelling and properly identify persons and places. Court reporters are also responsible for developing ways to store and retrieve their files. Stenographic and voice writing reporters also create and update the working dictionaries they use to convert their keystroke codes or voice files into written text.

Most court reporters work for state and local governments in courts, legislatures, and government agencies. Others work in home offices as freelancers. An increasing number work in four areas: *broadcast captioners* for television networks or cable networks for news, sports, and other events; *webcasters* for corporations, recording and making instant transcriptions of company sales conferences and the like; *Internet streaming text providers*, who post text via a live feed to the Web; and *CART reporters*, who specialize in working with the deaf using a system called Communication Access Real-time Translation, or CART.

Essential Gear

Learn all about it. In addition to listing certified schools that teach court reporting, the National Court Reporters Association Web site also offers an extensive Virtual Mentors program that matches experienced court reporters by specialty with students. The site also has links to descriptive articles on such specialties as captioner, CART provider, legal videographer, and freelancer. http://www.ncraonline.org

It can take anywhere from less than a year to almost three years to become a court reporter, depending on the type of specialization chosen. You can become a novice voice reporter in less than a year, but it takes almost three years to become a real-time stenotypist. There are about 130 vocational and technical schools and colleges where you train as a court reporter, but the National Court Reporters Association (NCRA) certifies only about half of these institutions. To find a school in your area, go to the NCRA Web site and type *certified schools* in the search bar. Under Search Results, click on Certified Schools. Schools are listed by state. Note the Program Key abbreviations that stand for the type of degree or program.

After completing a degree or program, some states require you to pass a test to become a court reporter or voice writer. Other states accept certification by the NCRA instead of state licensure. NCRA currently offers seven different nonsupervisory certifications to court reporters, including voice writer, captioner, CART provider, and video specialist. States that permit the voice writing method of court reporting accept voice-writing certificates. Go to http://ncraonline.org/certification/Certification for details on each certificate.

A shortage of court reporters and shrinking funds with which to pay them has caused some courts, particularly in civil cases, to switch to audiotape recording machines. Electronic court reporters and transcribers monitor and maintain these machines. They also often turn the audiotapes into official written legal transcripts and proceedings. Voice writers have also made significant inroads into the world of court reporting. Yet many courtrooms, especially in felony cases, still permit only stenotypists to record their trials and proceedings.

Essential Gear

Get the scoop on electronic court reporting. The Web site of the American Association of Electronic Reporters and Transcribers has helpful descriptions of the skills required, a comparison chart of different methods of court reporting, and a pull-down menu (under "Resources") with links to specific job listings by state and specialized dictionaries of legal, medical, and technical terms. http://www.aaert.org

Overall, the future looks bright for courtroom reporters. Job growth is expected to reach 25 percent—much faster than the average for all occupations between 2006 and 2016. The upward trend is

due not only to the increasing numbers of civil and criminal cases, but also to the increasing need for broadcast captioners, webcasters, Internet streaming text providers, and CART reporters in noncourtroom settings. Like those medieval clerics with their robes and tonsures, all these modern-day court reporters still have a significant place in society. They just wear different clothes to work.

You Are Here

Determine the depth of your aptitude and interest in becoming a skilled court reporter.

Do you find satisfaction in producing quick and accurate written records of events? Your manual dexterity, speed, and knowledge of grammar, spelling, punctuation, and vocabulary can serve you well as a court reporter, whether you work for the judicial branch of government, or for a broadcasting or cable network, Internet service provider, webcast producer, or provider of services to the deaf.

Navigating the Terrain

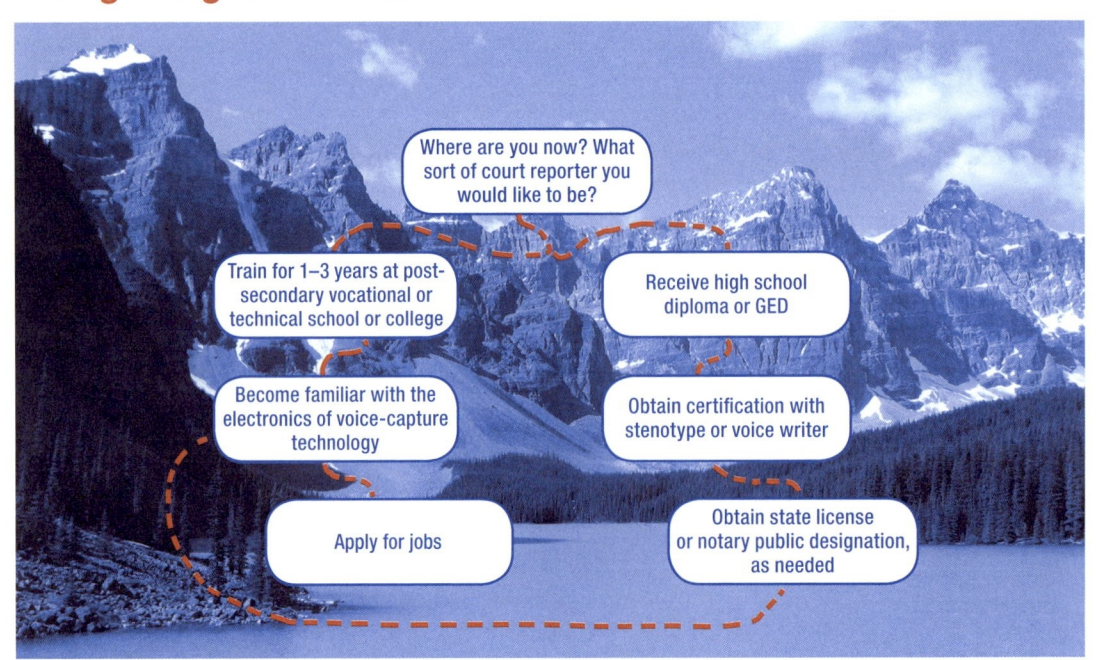

- Where are you now? What sort of court reporter you would like to be?
- Train for 1–3 years at post-secondary vocational or technical school or college
- Receive high school diploma or GED
- Become familiar with the electronics of voice-capture technology
- Obtain certification with stenotype or voice writer
- Apply for jobs
- Obtain state license or notary public designation, as needed

Can you commit yourself to the values of the organization(s) you serve, whether they are court systems, broadcasters, webcasters, or other providers? No matter where you work, your job will demand high concentration and attention to the details of the assignment. This level of awareness can best come from individuals who share the values of the organization(s) for which they work.

Do you have the flexibility to learn new technologies in order to qualify for different niches within court reporting? Since the fastest growing specialties in court reporting are new fields like CART, broadcast captioning, and webcasting services, those who can master these fields may have a better chance of getting a job. Those seeking work as stenographic typists are also highly sought after since fewer people currently enter this profession.

Organizing Your Expedition

Before you begin your adventure, consider the different places you might end up.

Decide on a destination. If you have had some school experience in audio recording devices, manual transcribing, or both, consider in which area you feel more comfortable. If you were the outstanding typist in your high school secretarial class, you may incline toward becoming a stenographic reporter. If you were the techie who was always busy at the college radio station or in the theater, you may gravitate toward becoming an electronic reporter. Are your manual and auditory skills both good? Then some jobs like voice writer may be more up your alley. Read up on each type of reporting, using the suggestions under Essential Gear and Further Resources, and decide which field feels most comfortable to you.

Scout the terrain. If you are interested in working in the court system, find out which courts use the different types of reporting (electronic, stenographic, voice writing) and observe parts of trials in which each type is used. This experience will give you a good idea of how the court reporter fits into the court system, and whether the trial atmosphere appeals to you. Do not be surprised if most actual trials are not as exciting as television courtroom dramas.

Notes from the Field

Aimée Suhie
Court reporter
New Fairfield, Connecticut

What were you doing before you decided to change careers?

I was an associate editor at a small daily newspaper (now defunct). I had to be at work at 5 A.M. and I worked straight through lunch so I could get home, take a nap, and be up when the kids got home from school.

Why did you change your career?

The schedule of my newspaper was leaving me pooped after about two years. I was still very much involved in my children's lives, church work, Girl Scouts, etc, and wanted to stay close to home yet still have a meaningful career. My sister had been a court reporter for about 10 years. I was reading John Grisham's *The Firm* in bed one night, when I turned to my husband and said, "I'm going to quit journalism and become a court reporter." He said, "Go for it." I gave a month's notice, signed up for the 21-month court reporting program, and we had no income from me (and the $12,000 that it cost for school plus supplies) for the next 21 months. I didn't make any real money until I'd been out of school for a year. Yet it was still the best decision I ever made!

If you are interested in working outside the courtroom as a captioner, webcaster, streaming content transcriber, or CART reporter, do a Web search for those terms, read up on the area(s) in which you are interested, and see if you can contact someone who is familiar with a specific area. One possible source of contacts is instructors or students at local educational institutions that offer courses in these areas.

Find the path that is right for you. Consider taking an introductory course in the area that most appeals to you at a local technical school or college. Your research, observations of a trial, and introductory course should put you on a clear path to pursue your passion to become a court reporter.

Go back to school. Even in electronic reporting, which usually requires no initial certificate, you may need eventual certification for some of the niches described above. Requirements for court reporter certification

How did you make the transition?

After the first three days of court reporting school, I walked out in a daze and said, "What have I done?" I really doubted I would ever finish school, let alone be a successful court reporter. But I was determined, and I discovered it was a true profession when I went to my first national NCRA convention in Washington, D.C. with my sister. I met some amazing women and men, and I saw the technological innovations that were just becoming well known.

What are the keys to success in your career?

Fortunately, the keys are exactly the same as in journalism. You must have an excellent grasp of spelling and grammar. You must be able to sit still and concentrate for hours at a clip without distracting others. You must use your time wisely. I use the trial breaks to check spellings and make up briefs (strokes that will easily define a phrase that is frequently used). You must be punctual. We make sure we arrive 20 minutes to a half-hour before the deposition begins to get set up and make sure everything is working. You should also be professionally dressed and never discuss the case with the parties. Last, you have to be organized, and have all your equipment ready to dash out the door should you get an emergency job on a morning when you expected to be off.

vary by state. Thirty-six states require either voluntary or mandatory certification. For up-to-date information, contact the United States Court Reporters Association.

Landmarks

If you are in your twenties . . . This is a good time do the coursework and obtain the certification necessary to enter this growing profession. A one- to three-year course at a postsecondary vocational school or colleges will put you in a position to fill any number of different niches in the court reporting spectrum of jobs, from traditional stenotypists to CART providers.

If you are in your thirties or forties . . . If your other responsibilities permit, a short-term course in voice writing, for example, will be helpful in finding jobs in this growing area. If you prefer a job with more flexible hours, virtually all of the specialties that hire staffers also employ freelancers who are paid either by the hour or by the job.

If you are in your fifties . . . It is never too late to enter this rapidly growing field. The number of cases on court dockets has swelled even as older court reporters are retiring, and the newer specialties are in high demand. Check the demand for specific jobs in your geographic area and consider taking a short-term course of study in the specialty that looks most attractive to you.

If you are over sixty . . . Your life experience, especially if bolstered by a related background in law, broadcast media, or work with the deaf, and your willingness to take an appropriate course of study, could make you stand out among other candidates.

Further Resources

The **National Verbatim Reporters Association** Web site lists NVRA-affiliated schools, mostly in the South, that teach verbatim reporting. On the "Resources Center" page, click on "Horace Webb Story" to read how the voice writing system was invented.   http://www.nvra.org

The **United States Court Reporters Association** represents verbatim court reporters who work in the federal court system. While many of its Web site features are open only to members, there are also lists of job openings and detailed job descriptions, answers to frequently asked questions, and examples of common errors made on the qualifying exam that is given to all aspiring federal court reporters.   http://www.uscra.org

Legal Aid Attorney

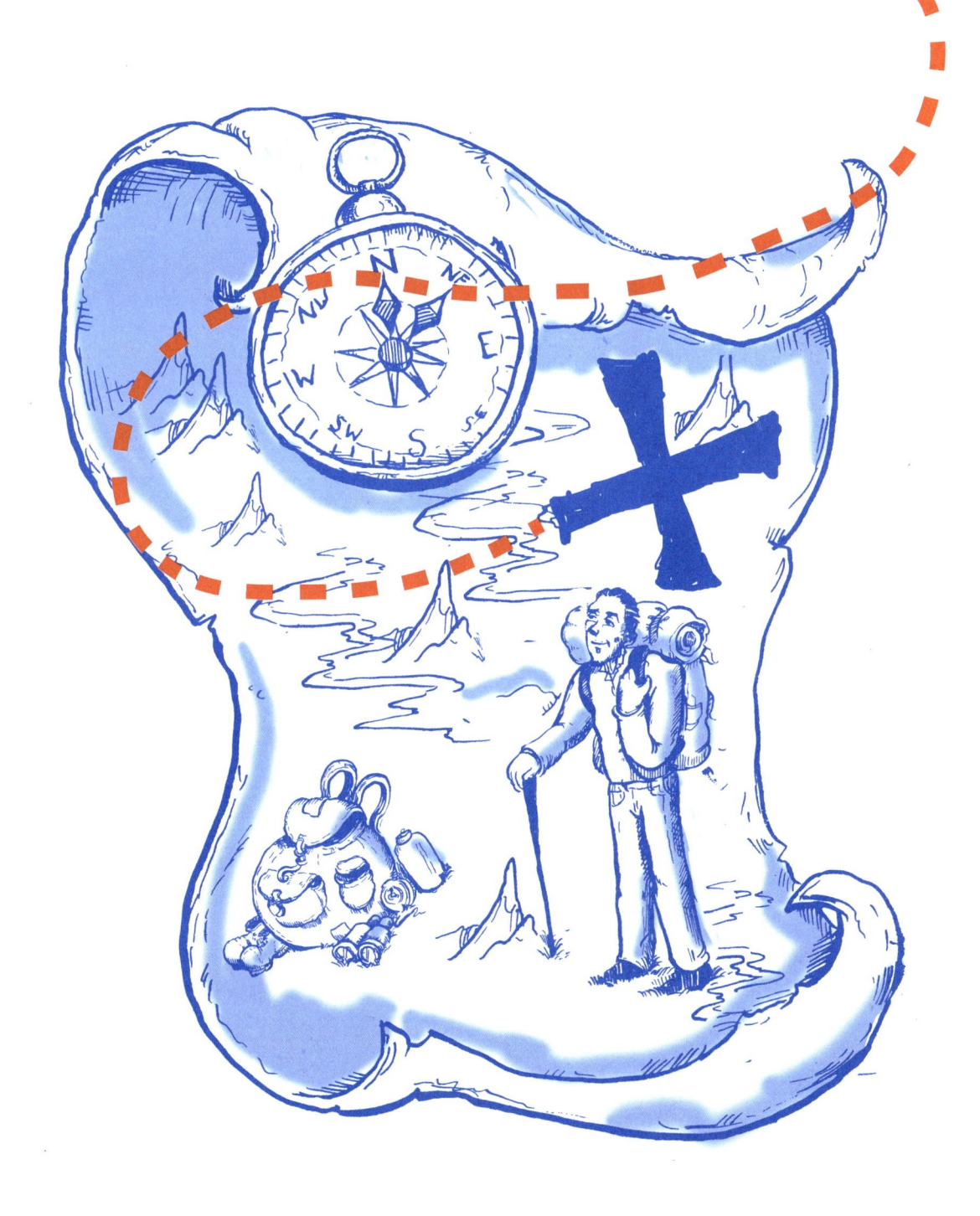

Legal Aid Attorney

Career Compasses

Balance the skills necessary to be a legal aid attorney.

Caring about the plight of your clients and making every effort to help them (30%)

Communication Skills to determine the facts of the case and the means that are available to solve the client's problem (25%)

Relevant Knowledge of the laws that apply to a particular case (25%)

Organizational Skills to prepare and present the most persuasive arguments (20%)

Destination: Legal Aid Attorney

"Equal Justice Under Law." These words appear over the entrance to the U.S. Supreme Court. They emphasize one of the basic concepts of law in Western civilization: Every citizen, no matter how humble, is entitled to the same legal rights. One of these rights, as spelled out in the Sixth Amendment of the U.S. Constitution, is "the right to have the assistance of counsel" in a trial. While challenged over the years, the Supreme Court has consistently backed the right to counsel, most famously in *Miranda v. Arizona* (1966), which extended the right to those being questioned by police after being arrested. Every faithful viewer of the television series *Law and Order* knows at least part of the famous "Miranda warning": "You have the right to remain silent. Anything you say can and will be used against you in a court of law. You have the right to speak to an attorney, and to have an attorney present during any questioning. If you cannot afford a lawyer, one will be provided for you at government expense."

Legal aid attorneys specialize in the defense of those who cannot afford a lawyer. As such, they put high value on the principles of serving others and promoting justice. "If you are thinking of entering the legal profession," advises the American Bar Association (ABA), "you should seek some significant experience, before coming to law school, in which you may devote substantial effort toward assisting others." The ABA aims that advice toward all would-be lawyers, but it would seem to apply especially to legal aid attorneys, for whom justice itself, rather than any great monetary gain, is often the main reward.

In order to fulfill the requirements of the Sixth Amendment, attorneys are encouraged to devote some of their time each year to pro bono defense of poor clients. Today some 1,600 agencies provide legal aid to such clients. In addition to government agencies like the Legal Services Corporation, these groups include charitable organizations, lawyers' associations, and law schools. In 2009, the American Bar Association released a study showing that 73 percent of its members contributed an average of 41 hours per year to pro bono work. Yet the ABA's committee on pro bono and public service estimates that "the poor still do not have access to the legal help they need 80 percent of the time."

All lawyers must successfully complete three years of law school and receive a J.D. degree. In addition, to practice law in a particular state or territory, one must pass a separate bar exam to be admitted to the bar of that jurisdiction. Admission is also usually subject to a background check. All of these conditions must be met for a person to be licensed to practice law. Those who have not passed the bar exam and yet represent

Essential Gear

Legal aid is on the way. The Atlanta Legal Aid Society has produced an eight-minute video, *Atlanta Legal Aid*, that gives a brief history of the organization, founded in 1924, and describes some of the cases it has handled, including brief interviews with the plaintiffs. The cases described in the most detail involve predatory mortgage lending and taking unjust advantage of the mentally handicapped. http://www.atlantalegalaid.org/themovie.htm

clients, prepare legal papers for a client, or claim to be an attorney are subject to prosecution for practicing law without a license.

A lawyer can enter the legal aid profession directly out of law school or after working in other areas of the law. Legal aid attorneys, like all lawyers, need to be able to work well with people and command respect from their clients and the general public. All attorneys need the persistence and reasoning ability to deal with complex cases and the creativity to deal with unique problems when they arise. The best legal aid lawyers also have a strong belief in the importance of defending the weak against the strong, and the just cause of the poor against the sometimes-corrupt power of the rich. The principle that one is innocent until proven guilty has long been a pillar of English law. The concept that defendants in a trial are entitled to legal defense, at government expense if necessary, is implicit in the Sixth Amendment to the U.S. Constitution.

Legal aid attorneys handle a wide variety of cases. These may involve housing, government benefits, immigration, employment, consumer protection, or disabilities, just to name a few areas. For example, in a single day in one large city legal aid office, interns and attorneys performed these tasks:

- seeking or appearing at hearings on behalf of clients either illegally evicted from their homes or wrongfully terminated from subsidized housing
- representing a client whose Temporary Assistance to Needy Families benefits were improperly reduced because of alleged failure to comply with welfare-reform work requirements
- documenting housing code violations to buttress a court case against a landlord

---

Essential Gear

Find a job in legal aid. The Web site of the National Legal Aid and Defenders Association features an extensive job search section that lists openings (including internships and fellowships) in civil legal and public defender organizations, pro bono and public interest organizations, and academia; a detailed history of legal aid (up to 2002); an e-library of articles submitted by readers; resources for civil legal aid attorneys and public defenders; and current news. http://www.nlada.org

☞ successfully advocating for a client whose Medicaid was terminated because she missed a recertification deadline while she was hospitalized

The demand for competent legal aid attorneys has probably never been greater than it is today. Deteriorating economic conditions have hit the poor disproportionately hard, forcing many into housing foreclosures, evictions, and bankruptcies that may require legal action. At the same time, government agencies have slashed funds that go to legal aid societies. Many attorneys with shrinking practices are tempted more than ever to shun the relatively less lucrative work of the legal aid attorney in favor of higher paid corporate work. Dedicated legal aid attorneys, however, believe in the importance of the Sixth Amendment and still rise to the challenge of providing "Equal Justice Under Law."

You Are Here

Your expedition as a legal aid attorney begins with your answers to several questions.

Am I firmly committed to the principal of equal access to the law by rich and poor alike? There is a reason the figure of Justice is shown wearing a blindfold. A person who appears in court—whether plaintiff or defendant—should be judged on the principles of the law alone, not by more visible factors like economic or social position in society. The legal aid attorney, too, should firmly believe in a society whose ultimate loyalty is to the law.

Am I willing to work for a smaller salary than that of my fellow attorneys in private or corporate practice? The compensation of legal aid attorneys is funded by a variety of sources, including charities, private donors, the federal government, and some state and local governments. These sources place restrictions on the kind of work a legal aid attorney can do. Their pay therefore cannot approach in size the large hourly fees that attorneys in corporate or private practice often earn. The legal aid attorney believes that upholding the principal of equality before the law is more important than the difference in remuneration.

Do I agree to advocate not just for my clients but also on behalf of the legal aid profession? While it is not a requirement of being a legal aid attorney, most legal aid professionals recognize the need to lobby the legal profession to fulfill its moral obligation to defend the poor. Despite the assurances of the Sixth Amendment, in the great majority of cases the weak and the indigent are represented by overworked lawyers who do not have sufficient time and resources to make the best cases for their clients.

Organizing Your Expedition

Before you set out, know where you are going.

Decide on a destination. An interest in providing legal aid can lead you in many directions. When you first set out, it may help to focus your interests if you can decide whether you are best suited to work on criminal, civil, or juvenile cases. Talking to someone at your local Legal Aid Society may help you make your decision. In criminal cases such as robbery, homicide, driving while intoxicated, and rape, an individual has been harmed. The defendant's guilt must be established beyond a reasonable doubt, and the penalty is imprisonment. In civil cases such as divorce, property disagreements, or contract disputes, an individual has also been harmed. Unlike criminal law, however, the penalty in civil cases is usually a monetary one and guilt is determined by a preponderance of the evidence presented. Juvenile law generally applies to persons under 18 years old, although adult courts can try juveniles if the judge in the case so rules. The main goal of juvenile justice is to rehabilitate children rather than punish them.

Scout the terrain. A law student exploring careers in legal aid may learn more about the criminal, civil, and juvenile justice systems in several ways. Many law firms offer internship and "summer associate" programs that pay law students to assist staff lawyers in researching and preparing cases. Since socially responsible attorneys regularly take on pro bono cases, interested law students can gain invaluable experience from assisting staff attorneys in these cases. Legal aid societies and other recipients of legal aid funding offer unpaid internships on civil, criminal, and juvenile law projects. These internships are usually available on a part-time basis

Navigating the Terrain

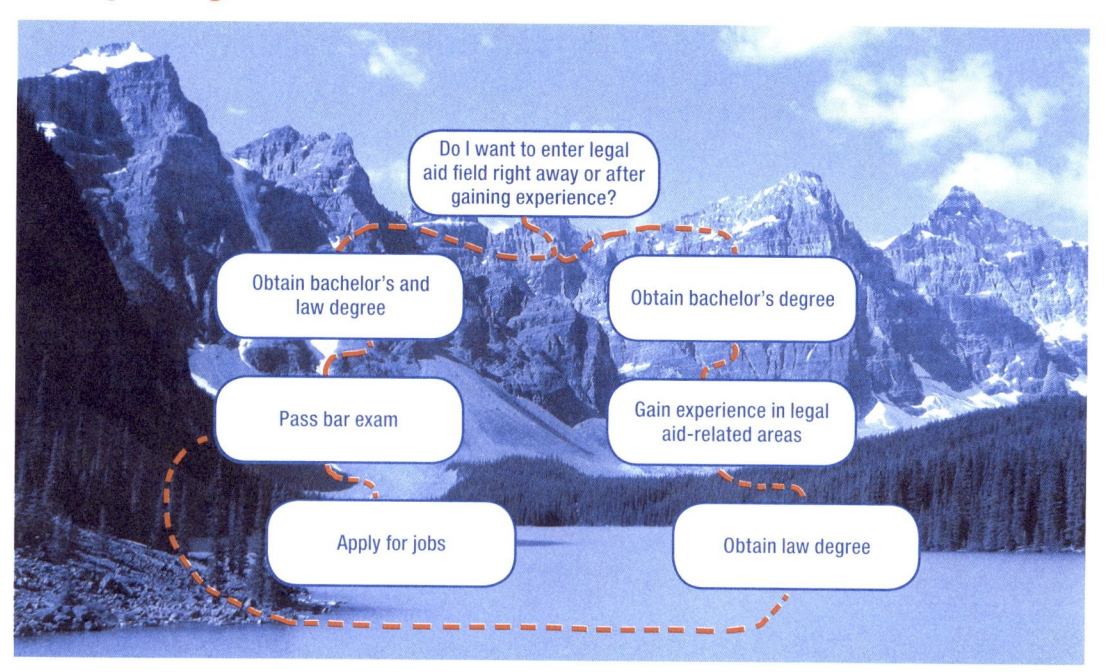

- Do I want to enter legal aid field right away or after gaining experience?
- Obtain bachelor's and law degree
- Pass bar exam
- Apply for jobs
- Obtain bachelor's degree
- Gain experience in legal aid-related areas
- Obtain law degree

during the fall and spring, and full-time during the summer. The career services office at your law school can give you more information about internships, fellowships, and other opportunities. Internships in particular may also be important in determining your career path since many organizations later hire students who have successfully interned there.

Find the path that's right for you. Once you have taken part in one or more of these internship and volunteer jobs, you may have a much better idea of where your strengths and interests lie. Other areas of the law that you may wish to investigate include immigration and asylum, housing, human rights, employment, death penalty, prisoners' rights, disabilities, consumer protection, community economic development, government benefits, and law reform. There is no shortage of areas in which to explore your interest in a career in legal aid. At some later point in your career you may decide to specialize in one area. Now, however, is the best time to broaden your scope and investigate all areas that look interesting before choosing the one that excites you the most.

Notes from the Field

Mildred Whalen
Public defender
Brooklyn, New York

What were you doing before you decided to change careers?

I was working for the federal government in the Department of Agriculture, Food and Nutrition Service, Northeast Region. Basically, we monitored the administration of the food stamp program in New York and New England. We reviewed the state regulations to make sure they complied with federal regulations, and reviewed the state programs both at the capitals and in individual food stamp offices throughout the states. We were responsible for notifying the states when they were not in compliance with federal regulations, reviewing any changes they proposed to make to come into compliance, and setting up penalties if they failed to come into compliance after a certain period of time.

Why did you change your career?

I didn't find the work interesting after about five years. I also felt that the Reagan Administration was not interested in actually feeding peo-

Landmarks

If you are in your twenties . . . Even if you do not yet have your law degree but your educational expenses or loans are manageable, now may be the best time to pursue internships working for the Legal Aid Society or some similar organization that does pro bono work. This experience can prove invaluable when you are deciding which direction to take after you finish law school.

If you are in your thirties or forties . . . If you have gained work experience from "the other side of the desk" in a field like health care or housing, you may have an advantage when applying both to law school and for jobs in legal aid.

ple, and that our job had become finding ways to deny people food stamps and punish them and the states for simple errors in order to make them not want to be part of the program. I decided I wanted to go to Washington to work on policy to make the program more about feeding people. Robert Greenstein of the Center for Budget and Policy Priorities was my hero, and I wanted to work for him.

How did you make the transition?

It appeared that everyone who was working on policy at that time was a lawyer, so I decided to go to law school. I received a scholarship from Cornell, and I was able to quit my job and go to law school full time. While in law school I discovered that I really liked advocacy, so I decided to become a trial attorney instead of a policy person.

What are the keys to success in your career?

I'm not sure what they are aside from the personal satisfaction of feeling like I do a worthwhile job. I am a public defender in federal court. I occasionally win a case at trial, but generally I just try my best to make sure that people are treated fairly and compassionately by the courts and the prosecutors.

If you are in your fifties . . . You might be surprised to find the number of people who entered law school to begin a second career either after raising a family or rising as far as they wanted to in a related field like social work. As always, your life experience will count greatly in a field like legal aid where you are directly helping people from all walks of life.

If you are over sixty . . . As a seasoned and successful member of the workforce who may now be in a position to "give back" to society, after attaining your law degree you may find the psychic wages from contributing to the social good outweigh the monetary rewards from your previous jobs.

Further Resources

Access to Justice, by Deborah L. Rhode (Oxford University Press, 2004), surveys 3,000 lawyers and concludes that the United States is failing to fulfill its promise of legal aid to the nation's poor. She faults both the quality and the quantity of legal representation, noting that many lawyers assigned to represent the poor do not take their jobs seriously, and that only 1 percent of the nation's lawyers serve the poor. Rhode proposes ways to curb frivolous lawsuits, unnecessary expenses, and unaffordable remedies.

Pro Bono Net is a national nonprofit organization founded in 1998 to increase access to justice through use of the Internet and increased volunteer lawyer participation. Its members include nonprofit legal organizations, courts, and bar associations. Its platforms have been adopted in 30 states and regions, reaching about two-thirds of the lawyers and poverty population in the United States.   http://www.probono.net

Arbitrator, Mediator, or Conciliator

Arbitrator, Mediator, or Conciliator

Career Compasses

Settle on the best skills mix to be an effective mediator.

Caring about the concerns of both sides in your mediation efforts (30%)

Communication Skills in order to reconcile your clients' positions (30%)

Relevant Knowledge of the law so your agreement will stand up (30%)

Organizational Skills to efficiently use your clients' time and resources (10%)

Destination: Arbitrator, Mediator, or Conciliator

Anyone who has read about, observed, or been a participant in a court trial knows that these proceedings can be expensive, lengthy, and not always satisfying. The adversarial atmosphere and the winner-take-all system may actually serve to extend the legal process, as one lawsuit may spawn appeals and countersuits. The lawyers are sometimes the only ones who come out ahead.

ARBITRATOR, MEDIATOR, OR CONCILIATOR

The alternative dispute resolution (ADR) process arose partly to improve this situation. Instead of suing each other, the two parties try to settle their differences out of court with the help of a third party. In arbitration, a third party called an *arbitrator* hears arguments and evidence from each side. The arbitrator then makes a decision (called an "award") that is usually binding—that is, both parties waive their right to a trial and agree to accept the arbitrator's decision as final. Arbitration is often used in commercial transactions, especially in international trade. Its use in consumer or employment cases, however, is more problematic. In these cases, individuals may not realize that by signing a contract they are usually giving up the right to sue in case of later disagreements. Instead, the consumer agrees to accept whatever the assigned arbitrator decides.

Mediation differs from arbitration in that the *mediator* helps the parties try to come to a mutually acceptable resolution but does not actually decide the dispute. Instead, the parties use the mediator's help to try to settle the dispute themselves. Mediation may precede arbitration or litigation. It is most useful when the parties want to preserve their relationship either as family members, business partners, or neighbors but need help in cooling the emotions that are preventing a resolution of the dispute.

Essential Gear

Read this classic. Roger Fisher and William L Ury's *Getting to Yes: Agreement Without Giving In*, 2nd ed. (Houghton Mifflin, 1991) propounds the now widely accepted thesis that negotiations should focus on *interests* rather than *positions*. Many training courses use or refer to this book.

Conciliation is like mediation in that the role of the *conciliator* is to help the parties reach a settlement. Conciliation differs in that the parties decide in advance whether they will be bound by the conciliator's suggestions. Conciliation often takes place in family law, and many psychologists and social workers as well as lawyers practice in this area. Their goal is to empower families to resolve conflict and protect children from the some of the hazards of the divorce experience. Since arbitration, mediation, and conciliation all require the same basic skills, the term *mediator* is often used to describe all three occupations.

Among mediators you will find lawyers, social workers, and mental health professionals as well as those with backgrounds in many other areas, including human resources and labor unions. As a mediator you will need speaking, critical thinking, and decision-making skills. Perhaps the most important skill, however, is to listen actively to what the parties are saying and make sure you understand the points they are making. It also helps to have a knack for being able to bring people together and forge compromises. Mediators usually work in offices or meeting rooms and may often have to travel, but some work from a home office. They work 35 to 40 hours a week except when contract negotiations require longer hours. Industries with the highest numbers of mediators are state and local governments, insurance-related activities, and professional, scientific and technical services. In 2008, these three sectors accounted for half the 10,000 mediators in practice.

There are no national training requirements for becoming a mediator, though some states have their own criteria. There is a trend, however, toward federal agencies and professional organizations offering their own training courses and credentialing programs. For example, the Federal Mediation and Conciliation Service (FMCS) offers a 40-hour training course to those with human resources or collective bargaining experience who wish to become federal labor arbitrators. For more information, go to http://www.fmcs.gov. The dispute resolution Web site Mediate.com offers a certification program intended as much for consumers and their advisers as it is for mediators as such. Requirements for certification include 100 hours of academic and training work, including at least a single 30-hour training and skills course in mediation. The Association of Family and Conciliation Courts does not offer a certificate course, but does provide two-day training programs in selected major cities on such issues as parenting, "high-conflict" families, and child custody. For more information, e-mail afcc@afccnet.org.

> ## Essential Gear
>
> **Read this book, too.** G. Richard Shell, *Bargaining for Advantage: Negotiation Strategies for Reasonable People*, 2nd ed. (Penguin, 2006). Outlines the six foundations of effective negotiations—your bargaining style, your goals, authoritative standards and norms, relationships, the other party's interests, and leverage—and how they affect the negotiation process.

The United States currently has more than 18 times as many lawyers per capita as Japan, and more than four times as many as the United Kingdom. While these statistics might seem to show a strong regard for

ARBITRATOR, MEDIATOR, OR CONCILIATOR

the law, they may also indicate an unhealthy overemphasis on litigation instead of the important democratic process of seeking compromise in common ground. The recent dramatic growth of alternative dispute resolution as a way of avoiding litigation is an encouraging sign of a significant change in the way we settle disputes. Here is a profession in which you can really make a difference.

You Are Here

Ask yourself these questions before you begin your expedition.

Do I have a strong desire to bring opposing parties together to forge agreements? As a mediator, you should have a firm belief in the effectiveness of mediation in settling disputes. You also need to have confidence in your own ability to hear each side fully and distinguish between more flexible and less flexible positions.

Navigating the Terrain

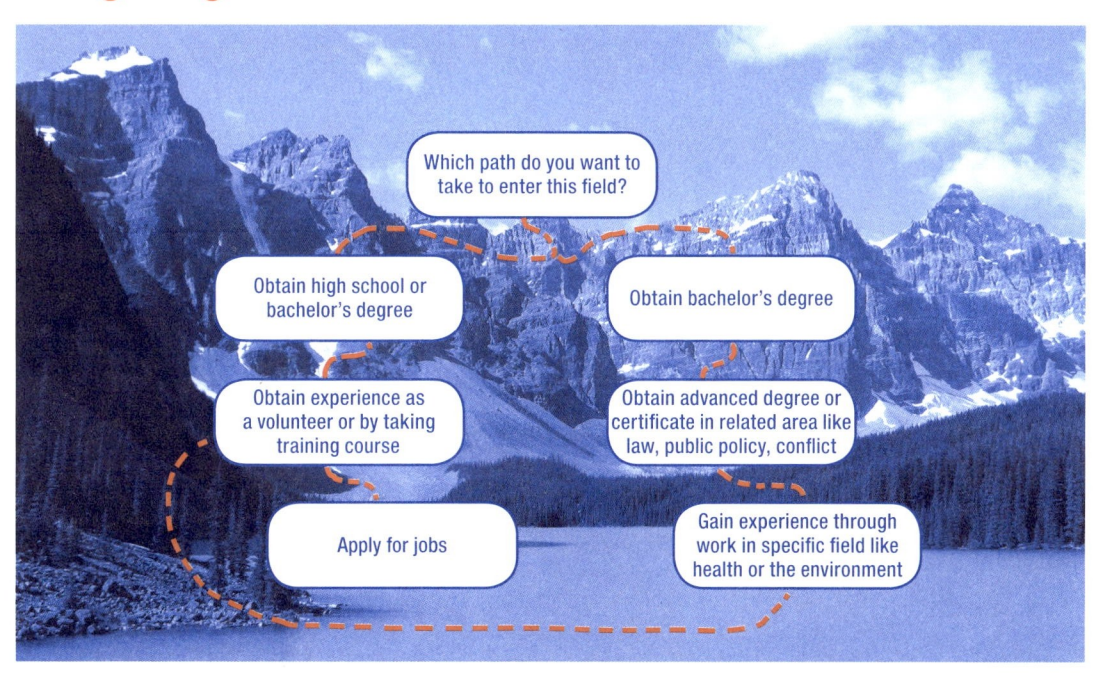

- Which path do you want to take to enter this field?
- Obtain high school or bachelor's degree
- Obtain bachelor's degree
- Obtain experience as a volunteer or by taking training course
- Obtain advanced degree or certificate in related area like law, public policy, conflict
- Apply for jobs
- Gain experience through work in specific field like health or the environment

Can I remain impartial when relating to parties who may be very different from me and from each other? A party's personality, background, or values should not cause you to be partial toward or against them. To maintain your objectivity as a mediator, you should neither give nor accept any item of value—whether it is a gift, favor, or loan—that could cause others to question your impartiality.

Can I avoid conflicts of interest or the appearance of such conflicts? Such conflicts can arise when the mediator has a past or present relationship, either personal or professional, that may raise a question about the mediator's impartiality. Mediators must scrupulously avoid such situations.

Organizing Your Expedition

Save time and trouble by knowing the different routes to your goal.

Decide on a destination. The techniques for bringing opposing parties together are similar in all fields, but you can hasten your journey if you have a good sense of the field in which you hope to practice, whether it is labor relations, commercial finance, the corporate area, construction, consumer affairs, insurance, the entertainment field, Olympic and professional sports, and so on. To find out more about some of these areas, go to the American Arbitration Association Web site and click first on "AAA University", then on "Reference Center". Your interests and life experience in the areas previously mentioned should help you gain either paid or volunteer experience in which you try out the skills you will need. These experiences will help you clarify your goal.

Scout the terrain. In furthering your education and employment experience, pick readings, courses, and jobs that will give you knowledge and experience in areas where mediation is used to settled disputes. For example, you will find a wealth of resources on the various aspects of dispute resolution on the American Bar Association Web site under http://www.abanet.org/dispute/resources.html. When looking for training courses, avail yourself of the ABA list of trainers (http://www.abanet.org/dispute/adr_training.html), which is organized by state. When looking for work, consider jobs that will expose you to the techniques of dispute resolution.

If you work in a unionized sector of the economy, for example, became familiar with the process of collective bargaining.

Find the path that is right for you. Initially, the abundance of different opportunities, and the many different paths you can take to realize them, may be confusing. Once you have taken advantage of the some of the many resources available to you, however, the path ahead should be clearer. Alternative dispute resolution is currently an increasingly popular way of avoiding litigation, and ultimately this popularity will work to your advantage. If you have a strong belief that conflict and dispute resolution is a key means of ensuring a stable society and preserving human resources, and you have invested your talent in both a training course and real-world experience, you are on the right track to reach your goal of becoming a successful arbitrator, mediator, or conciliator.

Landmarks

If you are in your twenties . . . Now is the time to clarify your job goals and gather related experience that will put you on a track to enter one of the many practice areas in this growing field. If you decide to take a short-term training course, choose carefully. You are generally wise to avoid online courses that lack actual face-to-face negotiation practice. Also make sure that the instructor's background includes hands-on experience as a mediator as well as theoretical knowledge.

If you are in your thirties or forties . . . If you have the time and resources to invest in an advanced degree and/or certification, this validation of your interest in mediation plus your real-life experience in related areas can give you an additional advantage in this growing job market.

If you are in your fifties . . . Your work experience in a related area like health and hospitals or business can provide a definite leg up when combined with a short-term training course or certification. The combination could propel you to the head of the line when seeking employment as a mediator.

If you are over sixty . . . If your résumé includes a variety of experiences—for example in both management and labor—you are probably

Notes from the Field

Larry Rute
Mediator
Topeka, Kansas

What were you doing before you decided to change careers?

My wife and I joined VISTA (Volunteers in Service to America) immediately following my graduation from law school. We were assigned to a VISTA low-income housing project with the Topeka Legal Aid Society. This proved to be the beginning of my 27-year legal services career culminating as Director of Litigation and Inside Counsel for Kansas Legal Services, our statewide legal services provider. In this role I was given the opportunity to litigate large and small cases, from administrative hearings to class actions.

In the early 1980s, judges in eastern Kansas announced that litigants in certain types of family law matters would be referred to mediation. In an effort to train young legal services attorneys regarding their role in the mediation process, I attended the first of many mediation-training programs.

In the mid-1990s, Kansas Legal Services received an endorsement from two state legislative committee chairs funding the first statewide employment discrimination mediation program with the Kansas Human Rights Commission. I served as the program's director. Soon thereafter the federal Equal Employment Opportunity Commission (EEOC) awarded Kansas Legal Services a similar contract. Both programs proved very

more qualified than most to be fair and impartial as a mediator once you have taken the standard 40-hour training course provided by the Federal Mediation and Conciliation Service, the Association for Conflict Resolution, or similar organizations.

Further Resources

The **American Arbitration Association,** has been a leading advocating of alternative dispute resolution since 1926. Their five divisions focus successful in resolving employment discrimination matters in Kansas and western Missouri.

Why did you change your career?

At the beginning of the millennium, I had served as a legal services attorney for 27 years. I had achieved many of the personal goals that I had originally set for myself when I first entered public service as a VISTA attorney. I felt that with my litigation and mediation experience, I was ready to take the next step as a full-time neutral.

How did you make the transition?

In 1999, I was contacted by a long-time professional friend who had served as a trial judge for 18 years and was interested in developing a new mediation/arbitration practice. At that time, there were no full-time mediators or dispute resolution neutrals in Kansas or western Missouri. We both had the advantage of having maintained excellent relationships within different segments of the legal community. I took the opportunity to wind down my responsibilities with legal services and established Associates in Dispute Resolution LLC.

What are the keys to success in your career?

In public service I followed the trial attorney's credo of learning the facts, knowing the law, and, whenever possible, out-working and out-hustling the opposition. Many of these same practice elements are indispensible to a successful mediation practice. It is particularly important for the mediator to be fully prepared and to work hard, during and after the mediation, to bring the matter to a successful conclusion.

on these kinds of disputes: commercial, construction, international, labor/employment/elections; and state insurance ADR disciplines. http://www.adr.org

The **Association for Conflict Resolution** is a membership organization devoted to "enhancing the practice and public understanding of conflict resolution." A student membership includes access to job notices and the opportunity to talk to fellow members in their interest section—for example, crisis intervention, international, or workplace. http://www.acrnet.org

Claims Adjuster

Claims Adjuster

Career Compasses

Appraise the requirements for succeeding as a claims adjuster.

Communication Skills to enable you to reach a successful settlement (30%)

Organizational Skills in planning and executing the work involved in handling a claim (25%)

Ability to Manage Stress involved when claims are disputed (25%)

Relevant Knowledge to apply to the specifics of each case (20%)

Destination: Claims Adjuster

There are over 319,000 claims adjusters, appraisers, examiners, and investigators today in the United States, and that figure is expected to increase 9 percent by 2016. Those numbers in themselves should suggest how big a role this job cluster plays in American life. Every time you make an insurance claim for a new drug prescription, disability, surgery, or auto or property damage or theft, one or more of the jobholders cited above may handle your claim. It is no wonder that claims adjustor is one of the top fifty in-demand occupations paying at least $20 per hour, according to the U.S. Department of Labor.

Claims adjusters, usually working for insurance companies, plan the work needed to handle a claim, consult with others to determine the extent of the insurance company's liability, and write a report that is used to judge the claim. Some, particularly in the medical field, have criticized insurance companies for unreasonably denying claims. For this reason, some claimants may prefer to hire a public adjuster who will work for their best interests rather than those of the insurance company.

Claims examiners perform duties very much like those of a claims adjuster, usually for life or health insurance companies. Claims examiners see that the rules have been followed in reviewing the claim. For example, hospital claims examiners check the claim form for accuracy and completeness, and compare the amount claimed with the average cost for similar diagnoses or average hospital lengths of stay for a particular treatment.

After they finish their review, claims examiners will either authorize payment or send the claim on to an *investigator* for further review. Insurance companies may call in investigators when there is suspicion of fraud—for instance, medical treatments that were never given or automobile "accidents" that were staged.

> ## Essential Gear
> **Learn the basics.** The Insurance Information Institute offers key facts about all types of insurance from the consumer's point of view. Their Web site includes a helpful glossary of insurance terms ranging from *accelerated death benefits* to *wrap-up insurance*, as well as free downloadable videos on the role of insurance in typical situations. http://www.iii.org

In cases of auto damage, an *appraiser* will usually estimate the cost of repairing the damaged vehicle. This estimate is then included in the claims adjuster's report. *Independent appraisers* often work from home rather than a company office. Advanced computer software valuation programs make working from a home office possible.

The following table summarizes the hours and work environment of the four occupations described above:

CLAIMS ADJUSTER

	Claims adjuster	**Claims examiner**	**Company appraiser**	**Independent appraiser**	**Investigator**
Work environment	Often in field	Usually in office	Often in field	Often work at home	Divided between field and office
Hours	Varied, according to location	Regular business hours	Regular business hours	Set own hours	Irregular

In general, jobs with the most regular hours are the least stressful, unless the work itself lacks variety and interest. The most stressful jobs are usually those in which a claim is questioned or fraud is suspected. In these cases, investigators may follow suspects to see if they engage in illegal acts or perform actions for which they have claimed a disability.

While there is no traditional educational requirement for these jobs, most employers prefer applicants with college degrees, including those with a background in vehicle repair (for appraisers) or law enforcement, interviewing, or interrogation (for investigators). Over 70 percent of those employed in the claims field have an associate's, bachelor's, or graduate degree. Many vocational and community colleges offer courses that include hands-on experience in auto repair and other occupations involving claims. Most beginners in the general field of claims adjustment work directly for insurance companies and receive on-the-job training while they gain experience working on progressively more complicated claims. Those interested in advancing in the field take continuing education courses to keep up with developments in their specialty. These developments include new laws and court decisions that affect the insurance industry, new drugs and medical procedures, or new car models and repair techniques. Employers may either train employees in these new developments or refer them to appropriate courses and seminars. Some of these courses are also available on the Internet. For more information on community colleges near you that offer courses and degrees in related fields like business, auto body technology, construction management, health care, and criminal justice, go to the Community College School Guide at http://www.collegebound.net.

The main qualification for working in this field is being able to communicate well with others, since claims adjusters frequently work with claimants, witnesses, and associates in the insurance field. Companies may test potential employees for their communications, analytical, and mathematical skills before hiring them. Knowledge of computer applications such as Fair Isaac Claims Advisor is also helpful. In addition to these skills, investigators need to be quick-thinking, determined, and forceful in their approach. Most companies prefer those with related experience, whether in law enforcement, the law, business or accounting, engineering or architecture, or medicine. Those with college degrees in related areas will have an edge, though most of these jobs have no specific degree requirements.

You Are Here

Before you begin your journey, ask yourself these questions.

Do I have a knack for making myself heard, listened to, and understood by others? In the claims business, you must be able to work closely with other insurance professionals as well as claimants and witnesses from all walks of life. Your ability to communicate with these people will be one key to your success.

Do I have a background in a field in which insurance claims are often filed? Knowledge gained in vocational school, college, or on the job in such areas as business, accounting, engineering, architecture, law enforcement, medicine, or auto repair will be helpful in seeking work in the insurance claims field. Additional training will also occur on the job, but prior experience will weigh in your favor.

Do I have a valid driver's license and a good driving record? You will need these for any job in the claims field that requires travel, such as claims adjuster or company appraiser.

Navigating the Terrain

- How will you become a claims adjuster?
- Obtain high school or GED diploma
- Gain experience in specialized area like auto repair or law enforcement
- Obtain optional training or certificate in your specialty area
- Apply for jobs

Organizing Your Expedition

Before you set out, imagine the kind of job that best fits your interests and experience.

Decide on a destination. Investigate what different kinds of claims workers do, where they work, and the skills and other qualifications needed for each job. It may help you to browse in the career sections of insurance company Web sites. For instance, Travelers Insurance, which employs 13,000 claims workers out of its more than 33,000 employees, features profiles of both a claims adjuster and an investigator on its Web site.

Scout the terrain. Use social and job networks such as Facebook and LinkedIn to find contacts in the insurance industry with whom you

Notes from the Field
Scott Copeland
Claims adjuster
Greenwood Village, Colorado

What were you doing before you decided to change careers?

I was working as a kindergarten teacher at a private school. I had worked as a preschool teacher during my college years, and was offered a position to teach the kindergarten program at a school where I had previously worked as a camp counselor during my holiday and summer breaks from school.

Why did you change your career?

I made the difficult decision to change careers for two reasons. The first was that I had a desire to work for a professional corporation with the chance for advancement. I had founded an online advertising company with some friends while in college, and I found myself missing the excitement of the business world. Unfortunately, the second reason is more obvious. It was difficult to make ends meet and still achieve my

could talk and who could answer your questions about jobs you are interested in. Browse the web, using key words like *insurance careers* and specific job titles like *claims adjuster,* and *claims appraiser, claims examiner,* and *claims investigator.* Follow up on Web sites—especially those of insurance companies—that provide further information on careers in claims work. Many educational institutions offer courses in claims work, either in traditional settings or online. In addition, many public libraries have sections on careers.

Find the path that is right for you. If you have done your homework, you should now have a good idea of the similarities and differences among the different types of work in claims. Consider how any of your courses in high school and/or college, plus your work experience, can provide you with a path into the insurance field. If your education and experience are appropriate, you may be qualified to enter a company training program. Here you may start out as a claims adjuster, but you goals of starting a family and becoming a homeowner while working at an educator's salary.

How did you make the transition?

The transition from working with five-year-old children on a daily basis to working in a professional environment was quite a challenge, but one I looked forward to. I have always attempted to face head-on the challenges presented to me, and I did the same with this situation. I had an initial learning curve like everyone else, and I had my share of failures, especially while learning the expected management style required to succeed with a major insurance carrier. I worked closely with my superiors. I continue to learn on a daily basis what it will take to continue my success in my current and future positions.

What are the keys to success in your career?

I believe the greatest key to my success at Travelers thus far is my willingness to work hard at being the best. If you are confident in your abilities, but are willing to pair that confidence with the humility and patience necessary to learn a new skill, it is my opinion that you can be successful at anything you work hard for.

will also be exposed to the whole range of choices in the claims field, as well as other aspects of insurance, and be even better prepared to find the path that is right for you.

Landmarks

If you are in your twenties . . . If you have either a high school diploma or a college degree, and some work experience in a related field, this is an ideal time to apply to either a local or national insurance company. Here you can train on the job in an entry-level position that could provide a steppingstone to higher-level positions.

If you are in your thirties or forties . . . Though competition can be strong in the insurance field, your longer work experience in a related field like health and hospitals may better qualify you to benefit from a company training program than the experience of a younger candidate.

If you are in your fifties . . . The claims field can be a good place for second careers for those who are retiring from fields like law enforcement or auto repair-shop management, or those who must split home duties with a working spouse. Your experience could provide a smooth transition to a job as a claims investigator or auto damage appraiser after training by an appropriate insurance company.

> ## Essential Gear
> **Find out who does what.** The American Institute for Chartered Property Casualty Underwriters offers up to 20 professional designations from Associate in Claims to Chartered Property Casualty Underwriter, plus introductory programs in the same areas. Exams are administered online at http://www.ceu.com and http://www.aicpcu.org.

If you are over sixty . . . If you are ready for a change of career field, your life and work experience in a related field like auto repair or law enforcement will stand you in good stead when seeking work as an insurance adjuster, appraiser, or investigator.

Further Resources

According to its Web site, the **International Claim Association** "provides a forum for information exchange and a program of education" to its members, which include life and health insurance companies. Online, proctored exams measure members' knowledge in a variety of areas.   http://www.claim.org

The **Life Office Management Association** (LOMA) is a 1200-member organization founded in 1924 to engage in research and educational activities and to improve member company operations. LOMA companies account for about 95 percent of all life insurance currently in force in the United States. LOMA offers over 100 self-study courses in life insurance, customer service, and more, using prize-winning textbooks that can be ordered online, plus about 120 short-term, online courses in the same areas.   http://www.loma.org

Appendix A

Going Solo: Starting Your Own Business

Starting your own business can be very rewarding—not only in terms of potential financial success, but also in the pleasure derived from building something from the ground up, contributing to the community, being your own boss, and feeling reasonably in control of your fate. However, business ownership carries its own obligations—both in terms of long hours of hard work and new financial and legal responsibilities. If you succeed in growing your business, your responsibilities only increase. Many new business owners come in expecting freedom only to find themselves chained tighter to their desks than ever before. Still, many business owners find greater satisfaction in their career paths than do workers employed by others.

The Internet has also changed the playing field for small business owners, making it easier than ever before to strike out on your own. While small mom-and-pop businesses such as hairdressers and grocery stores have always been part of the economic landscape, the Internet has made reaching and marketing to a niche easier and more profitable. This has made possible a boom in *microbusinesses*. Generally, a microbusiness is considered to have under ten employees. A microbusiness is also sometimes called a *SOHO* for "small office/home office."

The following appendix is intended to explain, in general terms, the steps in launching a small business, no matter whether it is selling your Web-design services or opening a pizzeria with business partners. It will also point out some of the things you will need to bear in mind. Remember also that the particular obligations of your municipality, state, province, or country may vary, and that this is by no means a substitute for doing your own legwork. Further suggested reading is listed at the end.

Crafting a Business Plan

It has often been said that success is 1 percent inspiration and 99 percent perspiration. However, the interface between the two can often be hard to achieve. The first step to taking your idea and making it reality is constructing a viable *business plan*. The purpose of a business plan is to think things all the way through, to make sure your ideas really are profitable, and to figure out the "who, what, when, where, why, and how" of your business. It fills in the details for three areas: your goals, why you think they are attainable, and how you plan to get to there. "You need to know where you're going before you take that first step," says Drew Curtis, successful Internet entrepreneur and founder of the popular newsfilter Fark.com.

Take care in writing your business plan. Generally, these documents contain several parts: An *executive summary* stating the essence of the plan; a *market summary* explaining how a need exists for the product and service you will supply and giving an idea of potential profitability by comparing your business to similar organizations; a *company description* which includes your products and services, why you think your organization will succeed, and any special advantages you have, as well as a description of *organization* and *management*; and your *marketing and sales strategy*. This last item should include market highlights and demographic information and trends that relate to your proposal. Also include a *funding request* for the amount of start-up capital you will need. This is supported by a section on *financials*, or the sort of cash flow you can expect, based on market analysis, projection, and comparison with existing companies. Other needed information, such as personal financial history, résumés, legal documents, or pictures of your product, can be placed in *appendices*.

Use your business plan to get an idea of how much startup money is necessary and to discipline your thinking and challenge your preconceived notions before you develop your cash flow. The business plan will tell you how long it will take before you turn a profit, which in turn is linked to how long it will before you will be able to pay back investors or a bank loan—which is something that anyone supplying you with money will want to know. Even if you are planning to subsist on grants or you are not planning on investment or even starting a for-profit company, the discipline imposed by the business plan is still the first step to organizing your venture.

A business plan also gives you a realistic view of your personal financial obligations. How long can you afford to live without regular income? How are you going to afford medical insurance? When will your business begin turning a profit? How much of a profit? Will you need to reinvest your profits in the business, or can you begin living off of them? Proper planning is key to success in any venture.

A final note on business plans: Take into account realistic expected profit minus realistic costs. Many small business owners begin by underestimating start-ups and variable costs (such as electricity bills), and then underpricing their product. This effectively paints them into a corner from which it is hard to make a profit. Allow for realistic market conditions on both the supply and the demand side.

Partnering Up

You should think long and hard about the decision to go into business with a partner (or partners). Whereas other people can bring needed capital, expertise, and labor to a business, they can also be liabilities. The questions you need to ask yourself are:

- Will this person be a full and equal partner? In other words, are they able to carry their own weight? Make a full and fair assessment of your potential partner's personality. Going into business with someone who lacks a work ethic, or prefers giving directions to working in the trenches, can be a frustrating experience.
- What will they contribute to the business? For instance, a partner may bring in start-up money, facilities, or equipment. However, consider if this is enough of a reason to bring them on board. You may be able to get the same advantages in another way—for instance, renting a garage rather than working out of your partner's. Likewise, doubling skill sets does not always double productivity.
- Do they have any liabilities? For instance, if your prospective partner has declared bankruptcy in the past, this can hurt your collective venture's ability to get credit.
- Will the profits be able to sustain all the partners? Many start-up ventures do not turn profits immediately, and what little they do produce can be spread thin amongst many partners. Carefully work out the math.

Also bear in mind that going into business together can put a strain on even the best personal relationships. No matter whether it is family, friends, or strangers, keep everything very professional with written agreements regarding these investments. Get everything in writing, and be clear where obligations begin and end. "It's important to go into business with the right people," says Curtis. "If you don't—if it degrades into infighting and petty bickering—it can really go south quickly."

Incorporating. . . or Not

Think long and hard about incorporating. Starting a business often requires a fairly large—and risky—financial investment, which in turn exposes you to personal liability. Furthermore, as your business grows, so does your risk. Incorporating can help you shield yourself from this liability. However, it also has disadvantages.

To begin with, incorporating is not necessary for conducting professional transactions such as obtaining bank accounts and credit. You can do this as a sole proprietor, partnership, or simply by filing a DBA ("doing business as") statement with your local court (also known as "trading as" or an "assumed business name"). The DBA is an accounting entity that facilitates commerce and keeps your business' money separate from your own. However, the DBA does not shield you from responsibility if your business fails. It is entirely possible to ruin your credit, lose your house, and have your other assets seized in the unfortunate event of bankruptcy.

The purpose of incorporating is to shield yourself from personal financial liability. In case the worst happens, only the business' assets can be taken. However, this is not always the best solution. Check your local laws: Many states have laws that prevent a creditor from seizing a non-incorporated small business' assets in case of owner bankruptcy. If you are a corporation, however, the things you use to do business that are owned by the corporation—your office equipment, computers, restaurant refrigerators, and other essential equipment—may be seized by creditors, leaving you no way to work yourself out of debt. This is why it is imperative to consult with a lawyer.

There are other areas in which being a corporation can be an advantage, such as business insurance. Depending on your business needs, insurance can be for a variety of things: malpractice, against delivery failures or spoilage, or liability against defective products or accidents. Furthermore, it is easier to hire employees, obtain credit, and buy health insurance as an organization than as an individual. However, on the downside, corporations are subject to specific and strict laws concerning management and ownership. Again, you should consult with a knowledgeable legal expert.

Among the things you should discuss with your legal expert are the advantages and disadvantages of incorporating in your jurisdiction and which type of incorporation is best for you. The laws on liability and how much of your profit will be taken away in taxes vary widely by state and country. Generally, most small businesses owners opt for *limited liability companies* (LLCs), which gives them more control and a more flexible management structure. (Another possibility is a *limited liability partnership*, or *LLP*, which is especially useful for professionals such as doctors and lawyers.) Finally, there is the *corporation*, which is characterized by transferable ownerships shares, perpetual succession, and, of course, limited liability.

Most small businesses are sole proprietorships, partnerships, or privately-owned corporations. In the past, not many incorporated, since it was necessary to have multiple owners to start a corporation. However, this is changing, since it is now possible in many states for an individual to form a corporation. Note also that the form your business takes is usually not set in stone: A sole proprietorship or partnership can switch to become an LLC as it grows and the risks increase; furthermore, a successful LLC can raise capital by changing its structure to become a corporation and selling stock.

Legal Issues

Many other legal issues besides incorporating (or not) need to be addressed before you start your business. It is impossible to speak directly to every possible business need in this brief appendix, since regulations, licenses, and health and safety codes vary by industry and locality. A restaurant in Manhattan, for instance, has to deal not only with the usual issues such as health inspectors, and the state liquor board, but obscure regulations such as New York City's cabaret laws, which prohibit dancing without a license in a place where alcohol is sold. An asbestos-abatement company, on the other hand, has a very different set of standards it has to abide by, including federal regulations. Researching applicable laws is part of starting up any business.

Part of being a wise business owner is knowing when you need help. There is software available for things like bookkeeping, business plans, and Web site creation, but generally, consulting with a knowledgeable professional—an accountant or a lawyer (or both)—is the smartest move. One of the most common mistakes is believing that just because you have expertise in the technical aspects of a certain field, you know all about running a business in that field. Whereas some people may balk at the expense, by suggesting the best way to deal with possible problems, as well as cutting through red tape and seeing possible pitfalls that you may not even have been aware of, such professionals usually more than make up for their cost. After all, they have far more experience at this than does a first-time business owner!

Financial

Another necessary first step in starting a business is obtaining a bank account. However, having the account is not as important as what you do with it. One of the most common problems with small businesses is undercapitalization—especially in brick-and-mortar businesses that sell or make something, rather than service-based businesses. The rule of thumb is that you should have access to money equal to your first year's anticipated profits, plus start-up expenses. (Note that this is not the same as having the money on hand—see the discussion on lines of credit, below.) For instance, if your annual rent, salaries, and equipment will cost $50,000 and you expect $25,000 worth of profit in your first year, you should have access to $75,000 worth of financing.

You need to decide what sort of financing you will need. Small business loans have both advantages and disadvantages. They can provide critical start-up credit, but in order to obtain one, your personal credit will need to be good, and you will, of course, have to pay them off with interest. In general, the more you and your partners put into the business yourselves, the more credit lenders will be willing to extend to you.

Equity can come from your own personal investment, either in cash or an equity loan on your home. You may also want to consider bringing on partners—at least limited financial partners—as a way to cover start-up costs.

It is also worth considering obtaining a line of credit instead of a loan. A loan is taken out all at once, but with a line of credit, you draw on the money as you need it. This both saves you interest payments and means that you have the money you need when you need it. Taking out too large of a loan can be worse than having no money at all! It just sits there collecting interest—or, worse, is spent on something utterly unnecessary—and then is not around when you need it most.

The first five years are the hardest for any business venture; your venture has about double the usual chance of closing in this time (1 out of 6, rather than 1 out of 12). You will probably have to tighten your belt at home, as well as work long hours and keep careful track of your business expenses. Be careful with your money. Do not take unnecessary risks, play it conservatively, and always keep some capital in reserve for emergencies. The hardest part of a new business, of course, is the learning curve of figuring out what, exactly, you need to do to make a profit, and so the best advice is to have plenty of savings—or a job to provide income—while you learn the ropes.

One thing you should not do is count on venture capitalists or "angel investors," that is, businesspeople who make a living investing on other businesses in the hopes that their equity in the company will increase in value. Venture capitalists have gotten something of a reputation as indiscriminate spendthrifts due to some poor choices made during the dot-com boom of the late 1990s, but the fact is that most do not take risks on unproven products. Rather, they are attracted to young companies that have the potential to become regional or national powerhouses and give better-than-average returns. Nor are venture capitalists endless sources of money; rather, they are savvy businesspeople who are usually attracted to companies that have already experienced a measure of success. Therefore, it is better to rely on your own resources until you have proven your business will work.

Bookkeeping 101

The principles of double-entry bookkeeping have not changed much since its invention in the fifteenth century: one column records debits, and one records credits. The trick is *doing* it. As a small business owner, you need to be disciplined and meticulous at recording your finances. Thankfully, today there is software available that can do everything from tracking payables and receivables to running checks and generating reports.

Honestly ask yourself if you are the sort of person who does a good job keeping track of finances. If you are not, outsource to a bookkeeping company or hire someone to come in once or twice a week to enter invoices and generate checks for you. Also remember that if you have employees or even freelancers, you will have to file tax forms for them at the end of the year.

Another good idea is to have an accountant for your business to handle advice and taxes (federal, state, local, sales tax, etc.). In fact, consulting with a certified public accountant is a good idea in general, since they are usually aware of laws and rules that you have never even heard of.

Finally, keep your personal and business accounting separate. If your business ever gets audited, the first thing the IRS looks for is personal expenses disguised as business expenses. A good accountant can help you to know what are legitimate business expenses. Everything you take from the business account, such as payroll and reimbursement, must be recorded and classified.

Being an Employer

Know your situation regarding employees. To begin with, if you have any employees, you will need an Employer Identification Number (EIN), also sometimes called a Federal Tax Identification Number. Getting an EIN is simple: You can fill out IRS form SS-4, or complete the process online at http://www.irs.gov.

Having employees carries other responsibilities and legalities with it. To begin with, you will need to pay payroll taxes (otherwise known as "withholding") to cover income tax, unemployment insurance, Social Security, and Medicare, as well as file W-2 and W-4 forms with the government. You will also be required to pay worker's compensation insurance, and will probably also want to find medical insurance. You are also required to abide by your state's nondiscrimination laws. Most states require you to post nondiscrimination and compensation notices in a public area.

Many employers are tempted to unofficially hire workers "off the books." This can have advantages, but can also mean entering a legal gray area. (Note, however, this is different from hiring freelancers, a temp employed by another company, or having a self-employed professional such as an accountant or bookkeeper come in occasionally to provide a service.) It is one thing to hire the neighbor's teenage son on a one-time basis to help you move some boxes, but quite another to have full-time workers working on a cash-and-carry basis. Regular wages must be noted in the accounts, and gaps may be questioned in the event of an audit. If the workers are injured on the job, you are not covered by worker's comp, and are thus vulnerable to lawsuits. If the workers you hired are not legal residents, you can also be liable for civil and criminal penalties. In general, it is best to keep your employees as above-board as possible.

Building a Business

Good business practices are essential to success. First off, do not overextend yourself. Be honest about what you can do and in what time frame. Secondly, be a responsible business owner. In general, if there is a problem, it is best to explain matters honestly to your clients than to leave them without word and wondering. In the former case, there is at least the possibility of salvaging your reputation and credibility.

Most business is still built by personal contacts and word of mouth. It is for this reason that maintaining your list of contacts is an essential practice. Even if a particular contact may not be useful at a particular moment, a future opportunity may present itself—or you may be able to send someone else to them. Networking, in other words, is as important when you are the boss as when you are looking for a job yourself. As the owner of a company, having a network means getting services on better terms, knowing where to go if you need help with a particular problem, or simply being in the right place at the right time to exploit an opportunity. Join professional organizations, the local Chamber of Commerce, clubs and community organizations, and learn to play golf. And remember—never burn a bridge.

Advertising is another way to build a business. Planning an ad campaign is not as difficult as you might think: You probably already know your media market and business community. The trick is applying it. Again, go with your instincts. If you never look twice at your local weekly, other people probably do not, either. If you are in a high-tourist area, though, local tourist maps might be a good way to leverage your marketing dollar. Ask other people in your area or market who have businesses similar to your own. Depending on your focus, you might want to consider everything from AM radio or local TV networks, to national trade publications, to hiring a PR firm for an all-out blitz. By thinking about these questions, you can spend your advertising dollars most effectively.

Nor should you underestimate the power of using the Internet to build your business. It is a very powerful tool for small businesses, potentially reaching vast numbers of people for relatively little outlay of money. Launching a Web site has become the modern equivalent of hanging out your shingle. Even if you are primarily a brick-and-mortar business, a Web presence can still be an invaluable tool—your store or offices will show up on Google searches, plus customers can find directions to visit you in person. Furthermore, the Internet offers the small-business owner many useful tools. Print and design services, order fulfillment, credit card processing, and networking—both personal and in terms of linking to other sites—are all available online. Web advertising can be useful, too, either by advertising on specialty sites that appeal to your audience, or by using services such as Google AdWords.

Amateurish print ads, TV commercials, and Web sites do not speak well of your business. Good media should be well-designed, well-edited, and well-put together. It need not, however, be expensive. Shop around and, again, use your network.

Flexibility is also important. "In general, a business must adapt to changing conditions, find new customers and find new products or services that customers need when the demand for their older products or services diminishes," says James Peck, a Long Island, New York, entrepreneur. In other words, if your original plan is not working out, or if demand falls, see if you can parlay your experience, skills, and physical plant into meeting other needs. People are not the only ones who can change their path in life; organizations can, too.

A Final Word

In business, as in other areas of life, the advice of more experienced people is essential. "I think it really takes three businesses until you know what you're doing," Drew Curtis confides. "I sure didn't know what I was doing the first time." Listen to what others have to say, no matter whether it is about your Web site or your business plan. One possible solution is seeking out a mentor, someone who has previously launched a successful venture in this field. In any case, before taking any step, ask as many people as many questions as you can. Good advice is invaluable.

Further Resources

American Independent Business Alliance
http://www.amiba.net

American Small Business League
http://www.asbl.com

IRS Small Business and Self-Employed One-Stop Resource
http://www.irs.gov/businesses/small/index.html

The Riley Guide: Steps in Starting Your Own Business
http://www.rileyguide.com/steps.html

Small Business Administration
http://www.sba.gov

Appendix B

Outfitting Yourself for Career Success

As you contemplate a career shift, the first component is to assess your interests. You need to figure out what makes you tick, since there is a far greater chance that you will enjoy and succeed in a career that taps into your passions, inclinations, natural abilities, and training. If you have a general idea of what your interests are, you at least know in which direction you want to travel. You may know you want to simply switch from one sort of nursing to another, or change your life entirely and pursue a dream you have always held. In this case, you can use a specific volume of The Field Guides to Finding a New Career to discover which position to target. If you are unsure of the direction you want to take, well, then the entire scope of the series is open to you! Browse through to see what appeals to you, and see if it matches with your experience and abilities.

The next step you should take is to make a list—do it once in writing—of the skills you have used in a position of responsibility that transfer to the field you are entering. People in charge of interviewing and hiring may well understand that the skills they are looking for in a new hire are used in other fields, but you must spell it out. Most job descriptions are partly a list of skills. Map your experience into that, and very early in your contacts with a prospective employer explicitly address how you acquired your relevant skills. Pick a relatively unimportant aspect of the job to be your ready answer for where you would look forward to learning within the organization, if this seems essentially correct. When you transfer into a field, softly acknowledge a weakness while relating your readiness to learn, but never lose sight of the value you offer both in your abilities and in the freshness of your perspective.

Energy and Experience

The second component in career-switching success is energy. When Jim Fulmer was 61, he found himself forced to close his piano-repair business. However, he was able to parlay his knowledge of music, pianos, and the musical instruments industry into another job as a sales representative for a large piano manufacturer, and quickly built up a clientele of musical-instrument retailers throughout the East Coast. Fulmer's experience highlights another essential lesson for career-changers: There are plenty of opportunities out there, but jobs will not come to you—especially the career-oriented, well-paying ones. You have to seek them out.

Jim Fulmer's case also illustrates another important point: Former training and experience can be a key to success. "Anyone who has to make a career change in any stage of life has to look at what skills they have acquired but may not be aware of," he says. After all, people can more easily change into careers similar to the ones they are leaving. Training and experience also let you enter with a greater level of seniority, provided you have the other necessary qualifications. For instance, a nurse who is already experienced with administering drugs and their benefits and drawbacks, and who is also graced with the personality and charisma to work with the public, can become a pharmaceutical company sales representative.

Unlock Your Network

The next step toward unlocking the perfect job is networking. The term may be overused, but the idea is as old as civilization. More than other animals, humans need one another. With the Internet and telephone, never in history has it been easier to form (or revive) these essential links. One does not have to gird oneself and attend reunion-type events (though for many this is a fine tactic)—but keep open to opportunities to meet people who may be friendly to you in your field. Ben Franklin understood the principle well—*Poor Richard's Almanac* is something of a treatise on the importance of cultivating what Franklin called "friendships" with benefactors. So follow in the steps of the founding fathers and make friends to get ahead. Remember: helping others feels good; it's often the receiving that gets a little tricky. If you know someone particularly well-connected in your field, consider tapping one or two less important connections first so that you make the most of the important one. As you proceed, keep your strengths foremost in your mind because the glue of commerce is mutual interest.

Eighty percent of job openings are *never advertised*, and, according to the U.S. Bureau of Labor statistics, more than half of all employees landed their jobs through networking. Using your personal contacts is far more efficient and effective than trusting your résumé to the Web.

On the Web, an employer needs to sort through tens of thousands—or millions—of résumés. When you direct your application to one potential employer, you are directing your inquiry to one person who already knows you. The personal touch is everything: Human beings are social animals, programmed to "read" body language; we are naturally inclined to trust those we meet in person, or who our friends and coworkers have recommended. While Web sites can be useful (for looking through help-wanted ads, for instance), expecting employers to pick you out of the slush pile is as effective as throwing your résumé into a black hole.

Do not send your résumé out just to make yourself feel like you're doing something. The proper way to go about things is to employ discipline and order, and then to apply your charm. Begin your networking efforts by making a list of people you can talk to: colleagues, coworkers, and supervisors, people you have had working relationship with, people from church, athletic teams, political organizations, or other community groups, friends, and relatives. You can expand your networking opportunities by following the suggestions in each chapter of the volumes. Your goal here is not so much to land a job as to expand your possibilities and knowledge: Though the people on your list may not be in the position to help you themselves, they might know someone who is. Meeting with them might also help you understand traits that matter and skills that are valued in the field in which you are interested. Even if the person is a potential employer, it is best to phrase your request as if you were seeking information: "You might not be able to help me, but do you know someone I could talk to who could tell me more about what it is like to work in this field?" Being hungry gives one impression, being desperate quite another.

Keep in mind that networking is a two-way street. If you meet someone who has an opening that is not right for you, but you could recommend someone else, you have just added to your list two people who will be favorably disposed toward you in the future. Also, bear in mind that *you* can help people in *your* old field, thus adding to your own contacts list.

Networking is especially important to the self-employed or those who start their own businesses. Many people in this situation begin because they either recognize a potential market in a field that they are familiar with, or because full-time employment in this industry is no longer a possibility. Already being well-established in a field can help, but so can asking connections for potential work and generally making it known that you are ready, willing, and able to work. Working your professional connections, in many cases, is the *only* way to establish yourself. A freelancer's network, in many cases, is like a spider's web. The spider casts out many strands, since he or she never knows which one might land the next meal.

Dial-Up Help

In general, it is better to call contacts directly than to e-mail them. E-mails are easy for busy people to ignore or overlook, even if they do not mean to. Explain your situation as briefly as possible (see the discussion of the "elevator speech"), and ask if you could meet briefly, either at their office or at a neutral place such as a café. (Be sure that you pay the bill in such a situation—it is a way of showing you appreciate their time and effort.) If you get someone's voicemail, give your "elevator speech" and then say you will call back in a few days to follow up—and then do so. If you reach your contact directly and they are too busy to speak or meet with you, make a definite appointment to call back at a later date. Be persistent, but not annoying.

Once you have arranged a meeting, prep yourself. Look at industry publications both in print and online, as well as news reports (here, GoogleNews, which lets you search through online news reports, can be very handy). Having up-to-date information on industry trends shows that you are dedicated, knowledgeable, and focused. Having specific questions on employers and requests for suggestions will set you apart from the rest of the job-hunting pack. Knowing the score—for instance, asking about the value of one sort of certification instead of another—pegs you as an "insider," rather than a dilettante, someone whose name is worth remembering and passing along to a potential employer.

Finally, set the right mood. Here, a little self-hypnosis goes a long way: Look at yourself in the mirror, and tell yourself that you are an enthusiastic, committed professional. Mood affects confidence and performance. Discipline your mind so you keep your perspective and self-respect. Nobody wants to hire someone who comes across as insincere, tells a sob story, or is still in the doldrums of having lost their previous job. At the end of any networking meeting, ask for someone else who might be able to help you in your journey to finding a position in this field, either with information or a potential job opening.

Get a Lift

When you meet with a contact in person (as well as when you run into anyone by chance who may be able to help you), you need an "elevator speech" (so-named because it should be short enough to be delivered during an elevator ride from a ground level to a high floor). This is a summary in which, in less than two minutes, you give them a clear impression of who you are, where you come from, your experience and goals, and why you are on the path you are on. The motto above Plato's Academy holds true: Know Thyself (this is where our Career Compasses and guides will help you). A long and rambling "elevator story" will get you nowhere. Furthermore, be positive: Neither a sad-sack story nor a tirade explaining how everything that went wrong in your old job is someone else's fault will get you anywhere. However, an honest explanation of a less-than-fortunate circumstance, such as a decline in business forcing an office closure, needing to change residence to a place where you are not qualified to work in order to further your spouse's career, or needing to work fewer hours in order to care for an ailing family member, is only honest.

An elevator speech should show 1) you know the business involved; 2) you know the company; 3) you are qualified (here, try to relate your education and work experience to the new situation); and 4) you are goal-oriented, dependable, and hardworking. Striking a balance is important; you want to sound eager, but not overeager. You also want to show a steady work experience, but not that you have been so narrowly focused that you cannot adjust. Most important is emphasizing what you can do for the company. You will be surprised how much information you can include in two minutes. Practice this speech in front of a mirror until you have the key points down perfectly. It should sound natural, and you should come across as friendly, confident, and assertive. Finally, remember eye contact! Good eye contact needs to be part of your presentation, as well as your everyday approach when meeting potential employers and leads.

Get Your Résumé Ready

Everyone knows what a résumé is, but how many of us have really thought about how to put one together? Perhaps no single part of the job search is subject to more anxiety—or myths and misunderstandings—than this 8 ½-by-11-inch sheet of paper.

On the one hand, it is perfectly all right for someone—especially in certain careers, such as academia—to have a résumé that is more than one page. On the other hand, you do not need to tell a future employer *everything*. Trim things down to the most relevant; for a 40-year-old to mention an internship from two decades ago is superfluous. Likewise, do not include irrelevant jobs, lest you seem like a professional career-changer.

Tailor your descriptions of your former employment to the particular position you are seeking. This is not to say you should lie, but do make your experience more appealing. If the job you're looking for involves supervising other people, say if you have done this in the past; if it involves specific knowledge or capabilities, mention that you possess these qualities. In general, try to make your past experience seem similar to what you are seeking.

The standard advice is to put your Job Objective at the heading of the résumé. An alternative to this is a Professional Summary, which some recruiters and employers prefer. The difference is that a Job Objective mentions the position you are seeking, whereas a Professional Summary mentions your background (e.g. "Objective: To find a position as a sales representative in agribusiness machinery" versus "Experienced sales representative; strengths include background in agribusiness, as well as building team dynamics and market expansion"). Of course, it is easy to come up with two or three versions of the same document for different audiences.

The body of the résumé of an experienced worker varies a lot more than it does at the beginning of your career. You need not put your education or your job experience first; rather, your résumé should emphasize your strengths. If you have a master's degree in a related field, that might want to go before your unrelated job experience. Conversely, if too much education will harm you, you might want to bury that under the section on professional presentations you have given that show how good you are at communicating. If you are currently enrolled in a course or other professional development, be sure to note this (as well as your date of expected graduation). A résumé is a study of blurs, highlights, and jewels. You blur everything you must in order to fit the description of your experience to the job posting. You highlight what is relevant from each and any of your positions worth mentioning. The jewels are the little headers and such—craft them, since they are what is seen first.

You may also want to include professional organizations, work-related achievements, and special abilities, such as your fluency in a foreign language. Also mention your computer software qualifications and capabilities, especially if you are looking for work in a technological field or if you are an older job-seeker who might be perceived as behind the technology curve. Including your interests or family information might or might not be a good idea—no one really cares about your bridge club, and in fact they might worry that your marathon training might take away from your work commitments, but, on the other hand, mentioning your golf handicap or three children might be a good idea if your potential employer is an avid golfer or is a family woman herself.

You can either include your references or simply note, "References available upon request." However, be sure to ask your references' permission to use their names and alert them to the fact that they may be contacted before you include them on your résumé! Be sure to include name, organization, phone number, and e-mail address for each contact.

Today, word processors make it easy to format your résumé. However, beware of prepackaged résumé "wizards"—they do not make you stand out in the crowd. Feel free to strike out on your own, but remember the most important thing in formatting a résumé is consistency. Unless you have a background in typography, do not get too fancy. Finally, be sure to have someone (or several people!) read your résumé over for you.

For more information on résumé writing, check out Web sites such as http://www.résumé.monster.com.

Craft Your Cover Letter

It is appropriate to include a cover letter with your résumé. A cover letter lets you convey extra information about yourself that does not fit or is not always appropriate in your résumé, such as why you are no longer working in your original field of employment. You can and should also mention the name of anyone who referred you to the job. You can go into some detail about the reason you are a great match, given the job description. Also address any questions that might be raised in the potential employer's mind (for instance, a gap in employment). Do not, however, ramble on. Your cover letter should stay focused on your goal: To offer a strong, positive impression of yourself and persuade the hiring manager that you are worth an interview. Your cover letter gives you a chance to stand out from the other applicants and sell yourself. In fact, according to a CareerBuilder.

com survey, 23 percent of hiring managers say a candidate's ability to relate his or her experience to the job at hand is a top hiring consideration.

Even if you are not a great writer, you can still craft a positive yet concise cover letter in three paragraphs: An introduction containing the specifics of the job you are applying for; a summary of why you are a good fit for the position and what you can do for the company; and a closing with a request for an interview, contact information, and thanks. Remember to vary the structure and tone of your cover letter—do not begin every sentence with "I."

Ace Your Interview

In truth, your interview begins well before you arrive. Be sure to have read up well on the company and its industry. Use Web sites and magazines—http://www.hoovers.com offers free basic business information, and trade magazines deliver both information and a feel for the industries they cover. Also, do not neglect talking to people in your circle who might know about trends in the field. Leave enough time to digest the information so that you can give some independent thought to the company's history and prospects. You don't need to be an expert when you arrive to be interviewed; but you should be comfortable. The most important element of all is to be poised and relaxed during the interview itself. Preparation and practice can help a lot.

Be sure to develop well-thought-through answers to the following, typical interview openers and standard questions.

- Tell me about yourself. (Do not complain about how unsatisfied you were in your former career, but give a brief summary of your applicable background and interest in the particular job area.) If there is a basis to it, emphasize how much you love to work and how you are a team player.
- Why do you want this job? (Speak from the brain, and the heart—of course you want the money, but say a little here about what you find interesting about the field and the company's role in it.)
- What makes you a good hire? (Remember here to connect the company's needs and your skill set. Ultimately, your selling points probably come down to one thing: you will make your employer money. You want the prospective hirer to see that your skills

are valuable not to the world in general but to this specific company's bottom line. What can you do for them?)
- What led you to leave your last job? (If you were fired, still try to say something positive, such as, "The business went through a challenging time, and some of the junior marketing people were let go.")

Practice answering these and other questions, and try to be genuinely positive about yourself, and patient with the process. Be secure but not cocky; don't be shy about forcing the focus now and then on positive contributions you have made in your working life—just be specific. As with the elevator speech, practice in front of the mirror.

A couple pleasantries are as natural a way as any to start the actual interview, but observe the interviewer closely for any cues to fall silent and formally begin. Answer directly; when in doubt, finish your phrase and look to the interviewer. Without taking command, you can always ask, "Is there more you would like to know?" Your attentiveness will convey respect. Let your personality show too—a positive attitude and a grounded sense of your abilities will go a long way to getting you considered. During the interview, keep your cell phone off and do not look at your watch. Toward the end of your meeting, you may be asked whether you have any questions. It is a good idea to have one or two in mind. A few examples follow:

- "What makes your company special in the field?"
- "What do you consider the hardest part of this position?"
- "Where are your greatest opportunities for growth?"
- "Do you know when you might need anything further from me?"

Leave discussion of terms for future conversations. Make a cordial, smooth exit.

Remember to Follow Up

Send a thank-you note. Employers surveyed by CareerBuilder.com in 2005 said it matters. About 15 percent said they would not hire someone who did not follow up with a thanks. And almost 33 percent would think less of a candidate. The form of the note does not much matter—if you know a manager's preference, use it. Otherwise, just be sure to follow up.

Winning an Offer

A job offer can feel like the culmination of a long and difficult struggle. So naturally, when you hear them, you may be tempted to jump at the offer. Don't. Once an employer wants you, he or she will usually give you a chance to consider the offer. This is the time to discuss terms of employment, such as vacation, overtime, and benefits. A little effort now can be well worth it in the future. Be sure to do a check of prevailing salaries for your field and area before signing on. Web sites for this include Payscale.com, Salary.com, and Salaryexpert.com. If you are thinking about asking for better or different terms from what the prospective employer offered, rest assured—that's how business gets done; and it may just burnish the positive impression you have already made.

Index

INDEX

A
ABA. *See* American Bar Association
administrative law judge (ALJ), xi–xii, 11–18
    age group landmarks, 17–18
    career compasses, 11
    education/training, 12, 15–16, 17
    essential gear, 12, 13
    federal, 12
    field notes, 16–17
    job description, 11–14
    licensing for, 13
    related work experience, 15–16
    resources, 12, 18
    skills/qualifications, 14–15
    specialization, 14–15, 16–17
    statistics on, 12
    transition expedition, 15–17
ADR. *See* alternative dispute resolution
age group landmarks
    administrative law judge, 17–18
    arbitrator/mediator, 81–82
    claims adjuster, 91–92
    court clerk, 54–55
    court officer, 45–46
    court reporter, 63–64
    lawyer, 7–8
    legal aid attorney, 72–73
    legal secretary, 36
    paralegal, 25–26
ALJ. *See* administrative law judge
alternative dispute resolution (ADR), 77
American Arbitration Association, 82–83
American Bar Association (ABA), 3, 8, 67
    paralegal training and, 22
American Independent Business Alliance, 105
American Small Business League, 105
arbitration, mediation v., 77
arbitrator/mediator, 76–83

    age group landmarks, 81–82
    career compasses, 76
    certification, 78
    education/training, 78, 80
    essential gear, 77, 78
    field notes, 82–83
    job description, 76–79
    resources, 82–83
    skills/qualifications, 78, 79–80
    specialization and, 80
    transition expedition, 80–81
Association for Conflict Resolution, 83
Association for Legal Career Professionals, 8–9

B
bailiff. *See* court officer
bailiff, origin of word, 40
bookkeeping, 101–102
Bureau of Labor Statistics, vii, viii, xi
business, starting own, 95–105
    bookkeeping for, 101–102
    building, 103–104
    employer in, being, 102–103
    field notes on, 109–110
    financial issues in, 100–101
    incorporation of, 98–99
    legal issues in, 99–100
    partnership in, 97–98
    plan, 95–97
    resources for, 105

C
career(s)
    finding new, vii–viii
    law/justice, xi–xvi
    successful, 109–118
career advancement, legal secretary, 32
career compasses
    administrative law judge, 11
    arbitrator/mediator, 76

INDEX

claims adjuster, 85
court clerk, 48
court officer, 39
court reporter, 57
lawyer, 2
legal aid attorney, 66
legal secretary, 30
paralegal, 20
certification. *See* licensing/certification
civil service exam
    court clerk and, 50
    court officer and, 43–44
claims adjuster, xiii, 85–92
    age group landmarks, 91–92
    career compasses, 85
    education/training, 87–88
    essential gear, 86, 92
    field notes, 90–91
    insurance terminology and, 86
    job description, 85–88
    job prospects, 85–86
    related work experience, 88, 90
    resources, 90, 92
    skills/qualifications, 88
    specialization and, 89
    transition expedition, 89–91
CLE. *See* continuing legal education
conciliation, 77
conciliator. *See* arbitrator/mediator
continuing legal education (CLE), xiii
    paralegal, 25–26
court clerk, xii, 48–55
    age group landmarks, 54–55
    career compasses, 48
    education/training, 49, 50
    essential gear, 49, 50
    field notes, 52–53
    job description, 48–50

    resources, 49, 55
    skills/qualifications, 49–50, 51
    specialization and, 53
    transition expedition, 52–54
court officer (bailiff), xii, 39–46
    age group landmarks, 45–46
    bailiff, origin of word, 40
    career compasses, 39
    education/training, 40–41, 43
    essential gear, 40, 41
    federal, 44
    field notes, 44–45
    job description, 39–42
    resources, 46
    salary, 40
    skills/qualifications, 40–43
    transition expedition, 43–44
Court Officers and Deputies Association, 46
court reporter, xii, 57–64
    age group landmarks, 63–64
    career compasses, 57
    certification, 59
    education/training, 59, 62
    essential gear, 58, 59
    field notes, 62–63
    job description, 57–60
    job prospects, 59–60
    related work experience, 61
    resources, 64
    skills/qualifications, 60–61
    specialization and, 58
    transition expedition, 61–63
cover letter, 115–116
credit, financing and, 100–101

D

DeVries, Mary A., 37

E

education/training, xiii–xiv. *See also* skills/quali-

INDEX

fications
- administrative law judge, 12, 15–16, 17
- arbitrator/mediator, 78, 80
- claims adjuster, 87–88
- CLE, xiii, 25–26
- court clerk, 49, 50
- court officer, 40–41, 43
- court reporter, 59, 62
- lawyer, 4
- legal secretary, 31, 32
- paralegal, 21, 22

elevator speech, 113
employer, starting own business as, 102–103
energy, 109–110
equity, business and, 100
essential gear
- administrative law judge, 12, 13
- arbitrator/mediator, 77, 78
- claims adjuster, 86, 92
- court clerk, 49, 50
- court officer (bailiff), 40, 41
- court reporter, 58, 59
- lawyer, 3, 4
- legal aid attorney, 67, 68
- legal secretary, 31, 32
- paralegal, 21, 22

experience, career success and, 109–110

F

FCCA. *See* Federal Court Clerk Association
Federal Court Clerk Association (FCCA), 55
federal employment
- administrative law judge, 12
- court officer, 44

field notes
- administrative law judge, 16–17
- arbitrator/mediator, 82–83
- claims adjuster, 90–91
- court clerk, 52–53
- court officer, 44–45
- court reporter, 62–63
- lawyer, 8–9
- legal aid attorney, 72–73
- legal secretary, 34–35
- paralegal, 26–27
- starting own business, 109–110

fifties, age group
- administrative law judges in, 18
- arbitrator/mediators in, 81
- claims adjusters in, 92
- court clerks in, 55
- court officers in, 46
- court reporters in, 64
- lawyers in, 7
- legal aid attorneys in, 73
- legal secretaries in, 36
- paralegals in, 25

finance, business and, 100–101
follow up, interview, 118

I

incorporation, 98–99
insurance terminology, claims adjuster and, 86
International Claim Association, 92
internships, legal aid attorney, 70
interview, 116–118
IRS Small Business and Self-employed One-Stop Resource, 105

J

job(s)
- changing law/justice, xv
- loss, vii
- offer, 118

job descriptions
- administrative law judge, 11–14
- arbitrator/mediator, 76–79

INDEX

claims adjuster, 85–88
court clerk, 48–50
court officer, 39–42
court reporter, 57–60
lawyer, 2–5
legal aid attorney, 66–69
legal secretary, 30–32
paralegal, 20–23
job prospects
    claims adjuster, 85–86
    court reporter, 59–60
    lawyer, 4
    legal aid attorney, 69
    paralegal, 23

L

Law School Admission Test (LSAT), 3
law/justice career, xi–xvi
    changing jobs and, xv
lawyer, xi, 2–9. *See also* legal aid attorney
    age group landmarks, 7–8
    career compasses, 2
    education/training, 4
    essential gear for, 3, 4
    field notes, 8–9
    job description, 2–5
    job prospects for, 4
    related work experience, 6
    resources for, 3, 8–9
    skills/qualifications, 3, 5
    specialization and, 5–6
    statistics, 2–3
    transition expedition, 6–7
legal aid attorney, xi, 66–74
    age group landmarks, 72–73
    career compasses, 66
    essential gear, 67, 68

field notes, 72–73
internships, 70
job description, 66–69
job prospects, 69
resources, 68, 74
salary/wages, 69
skills/qualifications, 69
specialization and, 71
transition expedition, 70–71
legal assistant. *See* paralegal
legal issues, business, 99–100
legal secretary, xii, 30–37
    age group landmarks, 36
    career advancement, 32
    career compasses, 30
    certification, 32
    education/training, 31, 32
    essential gear, 31, 32
    field notes, 34–35
    job description, 30–32
    resources, 36–37
    skills/qualifications, 33–34
    specialization, 34
    transition expedition, 34–36
The Legal Secretary's Complete Handbook. 4th ed. (DeVries), 37
licensing/certification
    administrative law judge, 13
    arbitrator/mediator, 78
    court reporter, 59
    legal secretary, 32
    paralegal, 22
Life Office Management Association (LOMA), 92
LOMA. *See* Life Office Management Association
LSAT. *See* Law School Admission Test

INDEX

M
mediation, arbitration v., 77
mediator, xii–xiii. *See also* arbitrator/mediator
microbusinesses, 95

N
NAALJ. *See* National Association of Administrative Law Judiciary
NAHO. *See* National Association of Hearing Officials
NALA. *See* National Association of Legal Assistants
NALP, 9
NALS. *See* National Association for Legal Professionals
National Association for Legal Professionals (NALS), 23, 26–27, 36
National Association of Administrative Law Judiciary (NAALJ), 18
National Association of Hearing Officials (NAHO), 18
National Association of Legal Assistants (NALA), 27–28
National Center for State Courts, 12
National Federation of Paralegal Associations (NFPA), 23
National Legal Aid and Defenders Association, 68
National Sheriff's Association, 46
National Verbatim Reporters Association, 64
networking, 110–112
NFPA. *See* National Federation of Paralegal Associations

O
Ohio Bailiffs and Court Officers Association, 46

P
paralegal (legal assistant), xii, 20–28
    age group landmarks, 25–26
    career compasses, 20
    CLE and, 25–26
    education/training, 21, 22
    essential gear, 21, 22
    field notes, 26–27
    job description, 20–23
    job prospects, 23
    licensing/certification, 22
    related work experience, 25
    resources, 22, 26–27
    skills/qualifications, 24
    specialization and, 21
    transition expedition, 24–25
Paralegal Assistant Today (magazine), 28
partners, business, 97–98
pro bono legal aid, 67

R
related work experience, xiv
    administrative law judge, 15–16
    claims adjuster, 88, 90
    court reporter, 61
    lawyer, 6
    paralegal, 25
resources
    administrative law judge, 12, 18
    arbitrator/mediator, 82–83
    business, starting own, 105
    claims adjuster, 90, 92
    court clerk, 49, 55
    court officer, 46
    court reporter, 64
    lawyer, 3, 8–9
    legal aid attorney, 68, 74
    legal secretaries in, 36–37
    paralegal, 22, 26–27
résumé, 114–115
    cover letter for, 115–116

INDEX

The Riley Guide: Steps in Starting Your Own Business, 105

S

salary/wages
    court officer, 40
    legal aid attorney, 69
sixties plus, age group
    administrative law judges in, 18
    arbitrator/mediators in, 81–82
    claims adjusters in, 92
    court clerks in, 55
    court officers in, 46
    court reporters in, 64
    lawyers in, 7–8
    legal aid attorneys in, 73
    legal secretaries in, 36
    paralegals in, 26
skills/qualifications. *See also* education/training
    administrative law judge, 14–15
    arbitrator/mediator, 78, 79–80
    claims adjuster, 88
    court clerk, 49–50, 51
    court officer, 40–43
    court reporter, 60–61
    lawyer, 3, 5
    legal aid attorney, 69
    legal secretary, 33–34
    paralegal, 24
    telephone, 112–113
Small Business Administration, 105
specialization
    administrative law judge, 14–15, 16–17
    arbitrator/mediator, 80
    claims adjusters and, 89
    court clerk and, 53
    court reporter and, 58

    lawyers and, 5–6
    legal aid attorney and, 71
    legal secretary, 34
    paralegal, 21
statistics, vii, viii, xi
    administrative law judge, 12
    lawyer, 2–3
    success, career, 109–119

T

telephone skills, 112–113
testimonials. *See* field notes
thirties/forties, age group
    administrative law judges in, 18
    arbitrator/mediators in, 81
    claims adjusters in, 91
    court clerks in, 54
    court officers in, 45
    court reporters in, 63–64
    lawyers in, 7
    legal aid attorneys in, 72
    legal secretaries in, 36
    paralegals in, 25
training. *See* education/training
transition expedition
    administrative law judge, 15–17
    arbitrator/mediator, 80–81
    claims adjuster, 89–91
    court clerk, 52–54
    court officer, 43–44
    court reporter, 61–63
    lawyer, 6–7
    legal aid attorney, 70–71
    legal secretary, 34–36
    paralegal, 24–25
twenties, age group
    administrative law judges in, 17
    arbitrator/mediators in, 81

claims adjusters in, 91
court clerks in, 54
court officers in, 45
court reporters in, 63
lawyers in, 7

legal aid attorneys in, 72
legal secretaries in, 36
paralegals in, 25

U

United States Court Reporters Association, 64

340.02373 G475   HFLOW
Gillam, Scott.
Law and justice /

FLORES
04/11